PARAGLIDING

FROM BEGINNER TO CROSS-COUNTRY

WITHDRAWN

David Sollom
Matthew Cook

Foreword by John Pendry

The Crowood Press

First published in 1998 by
The Crowood Press Ltd
Ramsbury, Marlborough
Wiltshire SN8 2HR

www.crowood.com

This impression 2005

British Library Cataloguing in Publication Data

A catalogue record for this book is available from the British Library.

ISBN 1 86126 044 X

Illustration acknowledgements
Many thanks to the following for supplying the photographs used in this book: Brauniger,
Andrew Bucknill, Michel Carnet – Sky Systems, Sarah Fenwick, Patrick Holmes – Edel UK,
Stuart Holmes, David Sollom and Emma Sollom.

Line drawings by Andrew Green

Typeset by Phoenix Typesetting, Ilkley, West Yorkshire.
Printed and bound in Great Britain by CPI Bath.

Contents

Foreword

During the past ten years I have seen paragliders develop from inefficient craft, little better than square parachutes, to today's modern wings, capable of travelling hundreds of miles. During this time, the skill level of pilots, especially those who, unlike me, have not come from a hang gliding background, has had to increase significantly to get the best from these gliders. At last now here is a book that will help pilots gain these skills, written especially with modern gliders and instrumentation in mind.

This book will be essential reading for both new and established pilots. It will help to refine the skills learnt during the pilot's initial training, as well as guiding him or her during those first, tentative steps towards cross-country flying. It also provides an excellent guide to those who have yet to sample this most exhilarating sport, giving a good indication of exactly how far paragliding has progressed since the mid-1980s.

David Sollom and Matthew Cook have amassed a considerable amount of flying and teaching experience between them. They have combined this into a book that is not only informative and interesting, but quite unique within the paragliding world.

John Pendry
Paragliding World Champion 1997
Former World, European and British
Hang Gliding Champion

Introduction

Paragliding has variously been described as 'the nearest thing to real flying', 'the simplest form of aviation yet invented', and 'an aircraft in a backpack'. It is also brilliant fun and has become an addiction for many people. It is especially popular in Europe, but its wonderful transportability has also allowed it to spread to many other, often remote, parts of the world.

Paragliding styles vary from country to country, largely because of differing weather conditions; for example, flying in continental Europe is predominantly concerned with big top to bottom distances, thermal lift and light winds, while in the UK pilots often fly in strong winds, off small hills, and often use ridge lift (or 'dynamic lift') to stay in the air.

A BRIEF HISTORY

Man has always been fascinated by flight, and has spent considerable time and effort trying to emulate birds. Those efforts ended in failure until someone (probably the ancient Chinese) forgot about flapping, and achieved progress with wings out straight. Straight wings and no other form of power enables gliding flight only, which is fine as long as you are happy to start high and end up low. When the Wright brothers stuck a small, inefficient power unit on to an established glider, things really began to happen.

Fortunately, a few people persevered with the idea of gliding flight, despite its limitations, and slowly developed gliders and gliding into the sports we know today. As well as understanding more about aerodynamics, and therefore making more efficient

Fig 1   Edel Superspace, an intermediate paraglider

gliders, these pioneers started to learn a lot more about meteorology, and soon learnt that, with skill and understanding, distance and duration flying was possible.

Over the years, gliders have developed into various different groups. At one end of the spectrum are the very high-performance, glass-fibre sailplanes, and at the other end

Fig 2 Airwave Black Magic dating from around 1989

are paragliders. All gliders use the same basic physics to stay in the air and cover distance, and the only real difference between them is the performance, and cost.

Paragliders are a development of the square parachuting canopies that appeared in the late 1960s. Initially, only the French and Swiss who lived in the Alps could fly these gliders, because the performance was very poor, and the Alps very steep. By the late 1980s, though, there had been sufficient progress that reasonable gliding performance was possible. At about this time, paragliding started to become more popular in the flatter European countries, including the UK. Since then, development has continued at a pace, both in performance and, more importantly, in safety.

GLIDING

The idea of the square parachute (and paraglider) is to use its forward speed to inflate an aerofoil wing, which in turn generates lift, and allows a slow, controlled descent. A good paraglider will sink at no more than one metre per second, at the same time travelling forwards at eight metres per second (approximately 15mph), giving quite a useful gliding performance. If you are able to fly your paraglider in air that is rising faster than one metre per second, the glider will rise with respect to the ground, despite it still sinking through the air. As long as the air keeps rising, so will you, until either the air stops or you fly out of the lift. This is the essence of gliding; a paraglider pilot needs a good understanding of meteorology, to be able to predict the location of any lift, as well as a basic understanding of aerodynamics.

ABOUT THIS BOOK

This book aims to be more than an introduction to flying paragliders cross country. It deals particularly with flying in the sort of conditions that predominate in the UK. It covers ground handling, flying in strong wind, and making the most of weak, often damp and soggy thermals, rather than covering vast distances around a mountain range, with thermals the size of football pitches leaping off every sunny slope.

If you are not yet a paraglider pilot, don't let this description put you off flying in the UK, where some of the best, most rewarding flying is to be had. Do be warned, however, that, due to the 'changeable' (the weather forecaster's euphemism for 'appalling') weather, days when good cross-country conditions exist are few and far between. It is therefore essential to maximize the potential of every day when you are able to get out and go flying.

This book has been written with two objectives: to provide a useful guide to accompany you during and after your paragliding tuition; and to answer some of the questions that hold pilots back from leaving the hill and flying cross country.

Fig 3 Nova Sphinx, a Performance paraglider

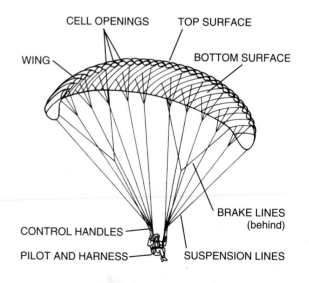

Fig 4 Typical paraglider

1   Basic Techniques

BASIC AERODYNAMICS

Flying has always occupied man's dreams, and his nightmares. The fear of falling is the biggest hurdle to overcome before you can feel relaxed enough in the air, both to learn how to fly, and really to enjoy your flying. An understanding of the physics of flight will certainly help you feel more at home in the air.

All heavier-than-air aircraft – paragliders, gliders or jumbo jets – make use of the same basic principle to stay aloft. This principle, the Bernoulli Effect, works in the following way.

Air is a fluid, similar to any other gas or liquid. If an aerofoil shape is passed through this fluid, the pressure will change around the aerofoil in a predictable fashion.

The pressure changes in two ways. The air that hits the underside of the wing has its pressure increased, because it is being hit by a solid object. The air that flows over the top side of the wing loses pressure, because the distance it has to travel over the top is longer than the distance travelled by the air going underneath. With lower pressure above and higher pressure below, the wing will tend to rise, and this is lift. In fact, more of the lift is generated by the reduction in pressure above the wing than by the increase below, by a ratio of approximately two-thirds to one-third.

The price to pay for this effect is drag. To keep generating lift, in order to stay up in the air, the wing must keep moving forwards through the air. There is always natural resistance to moving through the air, and this must be overcome. There are two ways in which designers do this: by putting an engine on the aircraft, or by arranging that, through the air at least, the aircraft keeps going

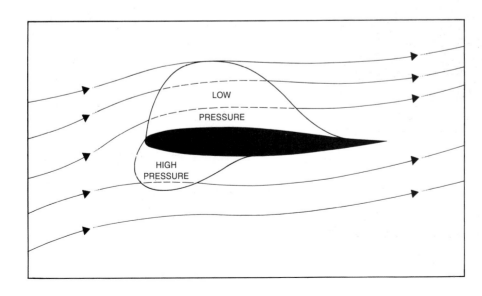

LOW PRESSURE

HIGH PRESSURE

Fig 5 Airflow and pressure around an aerofoil section

downwards as well as forwards. Paragliders are, of course, based on the second design.

UNPOWERED FLIGHT

When in flight, the glider wing has three forces acting on it: lift, the 'good' force that is holding it up; drag, the 'bad' force that is holding it back; and weight, which, in the absence of the other two, would bring the glider back to earth with a bump.

In order to overcome drag, it is necessary for the glider to be continually flying slightly downhill, using gravitational attraction to keep things going. It is similar to a bicycle without pedals; it soon rolls to a stop unless it is going downhill. The steepness of this slope is called the glide path or glide angle. Do not think, though, that when gliding you will be spending the whole time travelling from the top of a hill to the bottom. As long as the glider is dropping through the air, speed, and therefore lift, can be maintained. The art of gliding is to fly in air that is rising faster than the glider is dropping. This way the glider will, with respect to the ground, go upwards. This is a really fun thing to do, not least because the lift is totally free; there are no engines, no attachment to the ground, and you are using just the power of the sun and the wind.

Forces Acting on the Wing

Lift
As you can see in Fig 7, the lifting force does not act directly upwards from the wing, but is angled slightly forward as well. In fact, it acts at right angles to the direction of travel, which is logical when you think about it. The amount of lift generated by the wing depends on two things: the speed the wing is travelling through the air, and the amount of control input from the pilot. In the case of a paraglider, speed control is achieved by the use of flaps, which themselves generate lift when applied.

Drag
The drag that the wing generates will act directly against its direction of travel, so it appears to work backwards and slightly upwards. The amount of drag that the wing is producing is again dependent on both the

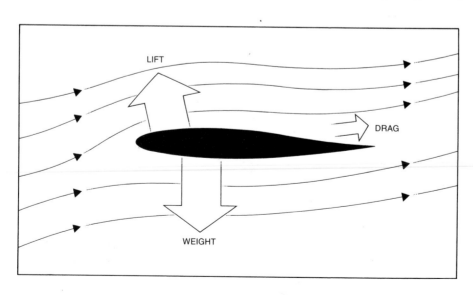

Fig 6 Distribution of forces

airspeed of the wing and the amount of control input by the pilot. The flaps are used for speed control work by generating drag.

Other than the logical sort of drag that the paraglider generates, the same kind that acts on a car or bicycle, trying to slow it down, there is also drag generated by the wing moving the air about as it produces lift. The first sort of drag, the air resistance, is called 'parasitic drag', and increases with the airspeed; the second sort, drag from lift generation, is called 'induced drag', and actually decreases as the airspeed increases.

Weight
The weight is the force that has to be overcome, or, more accurately, equalled, in order for the aircraft to stay up in the air. Most of the weight of the paraglider is the pilot, and this force is trying to pull him straight back towards the centre of the earth.

Although the weight is distributed over the whole aircraft, it can be said to act from a single point called the centre of gravity. The pilot is by far the heaviest component, and the C of G is pretty close to the centre of the pilot.

The Resultant
In order to overcome the force of the weight, the lift and drag forces on the wing must be equal to it, and work in the opposite direction. When these two forces are added together, the result is known as the 'resultant'. A stable paraglider is designed in such a way that, however the glider is flown, the lift and drag will always rearrange themselves so that the resultant is the same as the weight.

As with the weight, the resultant can be said to act from one point. This point is called the centre of pressure (C of P). Under normal circumstances, the C of P is at the centre of the wing.

GLIDING FLIGHT

Glide Angle

The glide angle of a glider is the same as the angle between the vertical and the lift vector. This slope depends on the amount of lift and drag that the wing generates. This is why the glide angle or glide ratio is often also termed the L/D ratio (for lift/drag). As the amount of lift or drag generated changes, for whatever

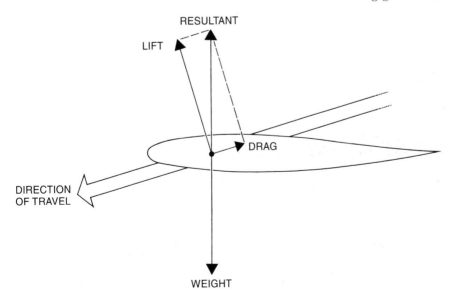

Fig 7 Lift, drag and weight vectors

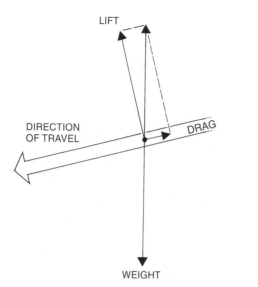

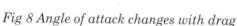

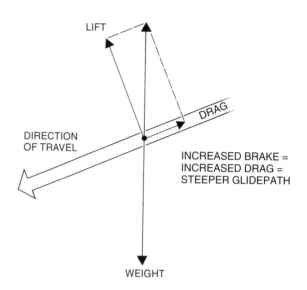

Fig 8 Angle of attack changes with drag

reason, so will the glide angle change. If the glider is flown in such a way that the drag is at a minimum, this normally results in the best achievable glide.

Angle of Attack

The angle of attack is the angle at which the airflow hits the paraglider's wing. The angle of attack can be altered during flight by operation of the brakes. The more the brakes are applied, the greater the angle of attack. This angle is critical to the way the glider flies, as the airspeed is dependent on the angle of attack, as well as the amount of lift produced by the wing.

The angle of attack can safely be altered within a set limit, and a safe speed range. Should this range be exceeded, at either too high or too low an angle, the paraglider will become unstable.

If the angle of attack is too high, the wing will stall (*see* Fig 11). This is when the smooth airflow over the top surface of the wing detaches and becomes turbulent and rotors.

Without a smooth airflow, the wing stops generating lift, generates lots of extra drag instead, and stops. Without lift, the wing will start to drop through the air, regaining forward speed, but losing considerable height as it does so. With sufficient ground clearance there is no big problem; under normal circumstances, flying close to the stall should be avoided completely.

If the angle of attack is too low, the wing tends to collapse (*see* Fig 12). The paraglider is a flexible wing, so if the air starts to hit the top of the wing, not the bottom, the lift will start to work downwards, and the wing will tuck underneath itself. This is not such a big problem as it might first appear, as it is quite difficult to reduce the angle of attack to dangerous limits. None the less, it is a concern and therefore covered in some detail later on in this book.

AXES OF MOVEMENT

While flying, any aircraft has three axes about which it can move – pitch (nose up and

Fig 9 Applying brake for directional control

down), roll (one wing tip up, one down), and yaw (one wing tip forward, one back). All aircraft, including a paraglider, need to be stable in all three axes.

Paraglider Control

Most aircraft control their direction of travel by directly controlling pitch, roll and yaw, but this is not the case with a paraglider. A paraglider uses a very simple system unlike that of any other sort of aircraft. Rather than using control surfaces (elevators, ailerons, rudders, and so on) to change the attitude of the aircraft in flight, it uses brakes to steer the wing, as well as control its speed, in much the same way as a tank or bulldozer.

The brakes are controlled by pulling down on a handle that is always held in the hands while flying. Pulling on the right hand one will slow down the right wing tip, pulling on the left will slow down the left tip, and pulling on both will slow the whole wing. There is no primary system for increasing the speed of the wing faster than the brakes off position.

As well as controlling the speed of the wing, the brakes also change the angle of attack, and thus the glide path (*see* Fig 15). As the brake is applied, so it will generate more drag on whichever part of the wing it affects. As the drag increases, so the glide path gets steeper, in order to maintain the correct relationship between lift and drag to counteract the weight. Thus, as both brakes are applied, so the angle of attack of the whole wing will increase.

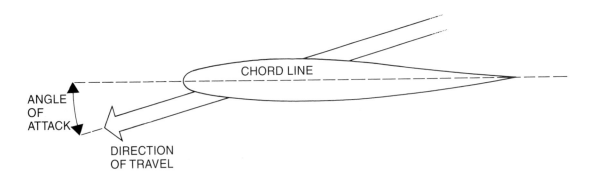

Fig 10 Angle of attack

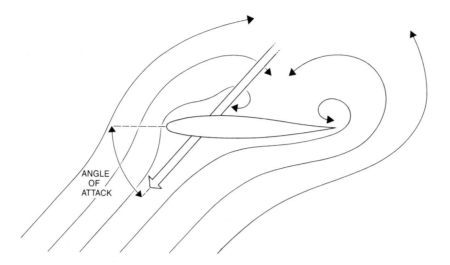

Fig 11 High angle of attack: stalled wing

Movement in Pitch, Roll and Yaw

The controls of the paraglider do not directly affect the attitude of the paraglider, but, due to the large distance between the C of G and the C of P, there is often movement, most noticeable in roll.

Roll movement occurs when one brake is pulled to turn the paraglider. As one side of the wing starts to slow, the glider will, initially, turn flat and begin travelling in a new direction. There is,

however, an appreciable amount of inertia attempting to keep the pilot travelling in the original direction. This departure in directions will roll the glider into the turn, amplifying the effect of the brakes.

Although smaller, there is a similar effect in pitch when both brakes are pulled together. This is a very important aspect of paraglider design, and has a direct influence on the way a paraglider is flown, especially when attempting to fly as efficiently as possible.

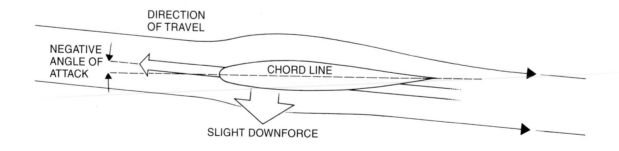

Fig 12 Negative angle of attack: collapsed wing

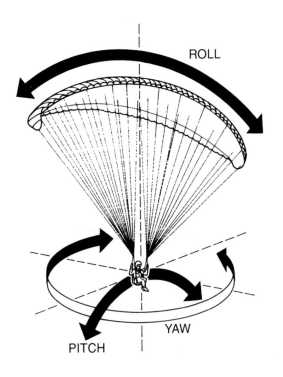

Fig 13 Axis of movement: pitch, roll and yaw

Paraglider Stability

Although the paraglider has no direct control in the axes of movement, it must be designed so that it is stable in all three. There are two distinct categories of stability. Static stability is the glider's ability to remain in a stable position, and dynamic stability is its ability to return to that stable state, however displaced (*see* Fig 16).

Pitch Stability
The paraglider's stability in pitch is derived purely from the vertical distance between the centre of gravity and the centre of pressure. As the wing is displaced, either nose up or nose down, so the pilot (who is basically the C of G) will try to swing back underneath the centre of the wing (which is basically the C of P). This is called pendulum stability (*see* Fig 17). The speed at which the pilot tends to swing will be directly related to the length of the paraglider lines. The shorter the lines, the quicker the swing.

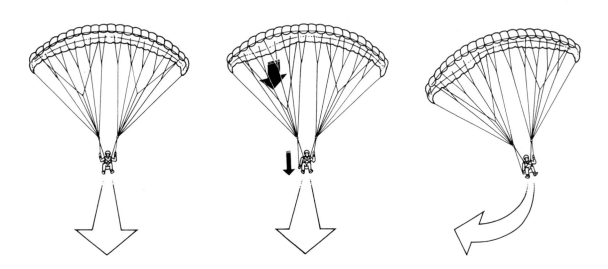

Fig 14 Turning a paraglider using brakes

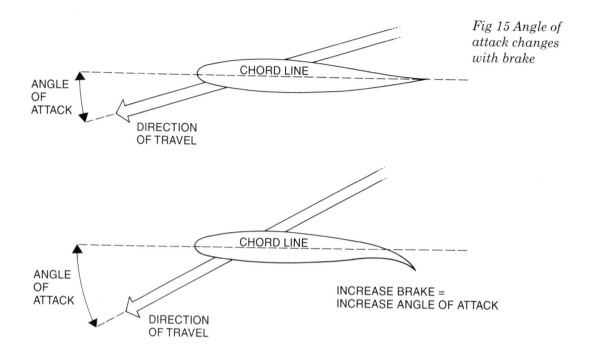

Fig 15 Angle of attack changes with brake

ANGLE OF ATTACK

CHORD LINE

DIRECTION OF TRAVEL

ANGLE OF ATTACK

CHORD LINE

DIRECTION OF TRAVEL

INCREASE BRAKE =
INCREASE ANGLE OF ATTACK

Roll Stability

Roll stability is virtually the same as pitch stability, relying on the pendulum force to return the pilot to a central position under the wing. Again, the length of the lines will have an effect on the roll speed of the paraglider. With longer lines, the glider will stay fatter in the turn; with shorter ones, it will roll more. Thus, line length will have a major influence on the handling 'feel' of the paraglider.

Yaw Stability

The yaw stability is derived from the curved shape of the wing, the position of the C of P in relation to the wing, and the fact that the wing is travelling through the air (*see* Fig 19). The degree of yaw stability in a wing is related to both the length of the lines (the longer the less stable), and the distance that the C of P is forward of the centre of the sail (the further forward, the more yaw stable). One of the most often noted problems with paraglider stability – the resistance to asym-

metric tucks – is related to the degree of yaw stability.

METEOROLOGY

Meteorology is the prediction of air movement and temperature/pressure changes, on anything from a local to a global scale. It is of great concern to all pilots, but especially to glider pilots, who try to predict lifting and sinking air, as well as the general weather.

Meteorology can be studied on two levels: small scale and large scale. Large-scale meteorology – the movement of air masses, fronts, low-pressure systems, and so on – is covered by a number of excellent flying meteorology books (*see* Further Reading), and only touched upon here. The prediction of air movement on a small scale, in front of and around a hill, for instance, which is called micro-meteorology, is covered in more detail.

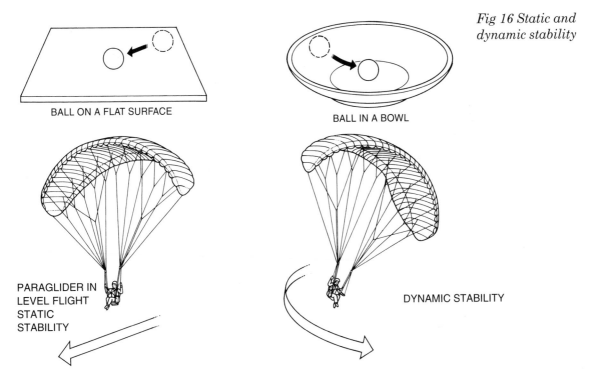

Fig 16 Static and dynamic stability

BALL ON A FLAT SURFACE

BALL IN A BOWL

PARAGLIDER IN
LEVEL FLIGHT
STATIC
STABILITY

DYNAMIC STABILITY

It must be remembered that meteorology is an inexact science. Words such as 'probably', 'might' and 'perhaps' are commonly used in weather forecasting, and it is a mistake to expect the weather always to do exactly what has been predicted.

Micro Meteorology

Air is a fluid, and behaves much like any other fluid, including water, when it flows over the ground. The difficulty with air is that it is invisible, so its behaviour cannot be seen; therefore, assumptions have to be made.

Airspeed
While we are flying, the paraglider is travelling forwards through the air. The speed at which the wing is passing through the air is called the airspeed. From the point of view of aerodynamics, the airspeed is critical. Lift generation depends directly on it, so it is important that a sufficient airspeed of around 10–25mph is always maintained.

Wind Speed
Almost every time we go flying, it is likely that the air will be moving across the ground. We know this as wind. A paraglider will be able to be launched in winds of between zero and 20mph. The speed that the air is moving over the ground is known as wind speed.

Ground Speed
As the paraglider travels through the air, and the air moves over the ground, the paraglider's speed over the ground will be a combination of the two. This is known as the ground speed. In the simplest case, when the paraglider is flying straight into the wind, then the ground speed will be the airspeed minus the wind speed.

The pilot must be able to visualize this

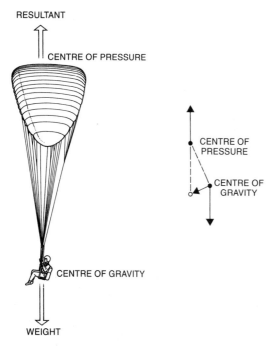

Fig 17 Pendulum stability in pitch

relationship between airspeed, wind speed and ground speed when flying, as it is important to be able to control the airspeed accurately with only the ground as a reference. Equally important is the realization of vertical movement, as the air through which the glider is flying moves up and down as well as horizontally over the ground. In this way, the glider can climb and sink at different rates, with relation to the ground, other than its normal sink rate, which is measured with respect to the air.

Airflow Near a Hill

Most flying, especially during the early stages of a flying career, will be in the lifting air immediately in front of a hill. If the wind is blowing against the hill, the air is deflected upwards over the top. If the hill is steep enough, and the wind sufficiently

strong, the air in front of the hill will be rising faster than the rate at which the glider is sinking. Thus, with respect to the ground, the glider will rise up to a height where the air is rising only as fast as the glider is sinking.

Fig 22 shows how the air behaves in various circumstances. In the area well away from the hill, at the left of Fig 22, the air is flowing horizontally across the ground. Closer to the ground, the wind will be slowed by friction; this is called the wind gradient'. This slowing is very important as it affects the way the pilot flies when approaching the ground. Whenever the wind is blowing there will be a wind gradient.

Fig 18 Gliding straight to join the thermal

Fig 19 Yaw stability

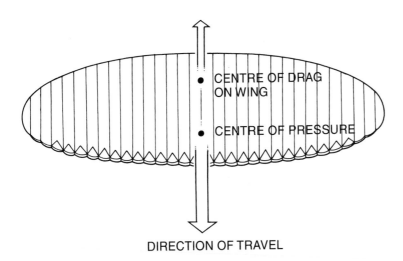

CENTRE OF DRAG
ON WING

CENTRE OF PRESSURE

DIRECTION OF TRAVEL

As the air hits the base of the hill, so it will be deflected upwards. The wind gradient will become squashed into a smaller area, next to the hill, and, if the wind is anything but square on to the hillside, the air will be deflected squarely up the slope. This is the effect of the wind gradient, and it gives the impression to those standing at the top of the hill that there is more lift than there actually is. As the air adjacent to the hill is deflected upwards, so it will affect the air above it, and it too will start to rise. This gives a fairly large area of lift, in front of and above the hill. The area is called the 'lift band'. The lift band is always in front of the hill, not above it, and the higher you go, the further forward the lift.

As the air starts to flow over the crest of the hill, so it starts to travel more horizontally again, with less and less lifting component. At the same time, the wind speed will increase, and this speeding up of the wind is

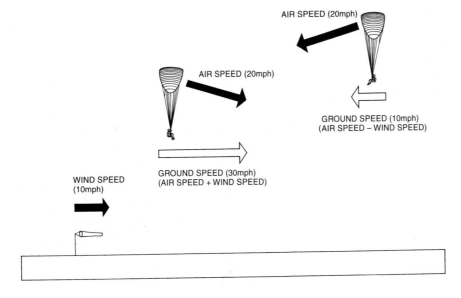

AIR SPEED (20mph)

AIR SPEED (20mph)

GROUND SPEED (10mph)
(AIR SPEED – WIND SPEED)

GROUND SPEED (30mph)
(AIR SPEED + WIND SPEED)

WIND SPEED
(10mph)

Fig 20 Air speed, wind speed and ground speed

Fig 21 Ridge soaring

known as the 'venturi' or 'compression'. The air flowing over the top of the hill is squeezed between the hill top and the faster-moving (thus higher-energy) air aloft. The term 'compression' is a little misleading; the pressure of the air is actually reduced by its movement over the hill, not increased. The effect is exactly the same as when air travels over the top surface of a wing. Any predictable air movement here is particularly important, as this is the area where take-offs and top landings occur.

THERMALS

Lift that occurs on the upwind side of a hill or slope is called 'ridge lift', and this is where the beginner to paragliding would expect to do most of his early soaring flights.

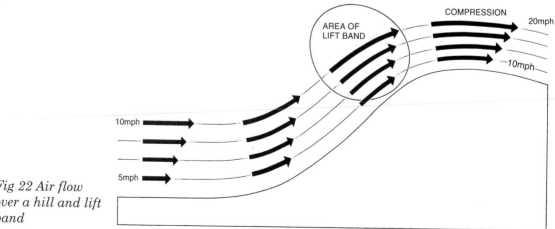

Fig 22 Air flow over a hill and lift band

The other form of lift commonly utilized, necessary for cross-country flying, is 'thermal lift'. The prediction and use of thermals is covered extensively later in this book; the basic weather necessary, and the make-up of the thermal itself, are as follows.

Turbulence

Turbulence occurs anywhere that air is not able to flow smoothly. The air, and therefore the turbulence, is invisible, so the only way to predict the existence of turbulence is to look for the causes of it.

Any solid object – from a small tree or bush to the hill or mountain from which we plan to fly – which disrupts the smoothness of the airflow, will generate turbulence in the form of rotors. These rotors will exist downwind of the obstruction for a considerable distance; the stronger the wind, the worse and wider-ranging the turbulence. The range of the turbulence will depend on wind strength as well as the size of the obstruction. As a very approximate guide, rotors could be expected within a distance of five times the height of the obstruction, assuming a noticeable wind. This is only a very rough guide – it is a good idea to keep as far away from any likely turbulence generator as you can.

One particular case should be mentioned, concerning the area immediately behind the hill from which you have flown. Most hills drop away on the back, and if you should get blown back, because the wind has become too strong, you must expect severe turbulence. This is especially the case on spine-back ridges and cliff sites.

Requirements for Thermals

Thermals are of particular interest to the pilot for two reasons: they provide an extremely useful source of lift, and they can generate some very noticeable turbulence.

On a general scale, the following three criteria have to be fulfilled if thermals are to be present. (Should any of the three be absent, it can be assumed that there is little chance of thermal turbulence.)

1. A heat source, almost always the sun. If the day is grey and fully overcast, it is very unlikely there will be any thermals, and almost certainly no usable ones.
2. Something to get hot. Miles of farmland or towns upwind from the flying site will generate thermals, while miles of sea will not.
3. Cold air aloft. This is where things get really interesting. The air inside the thermal will cool as it rises, because the pressure is decreasing. The

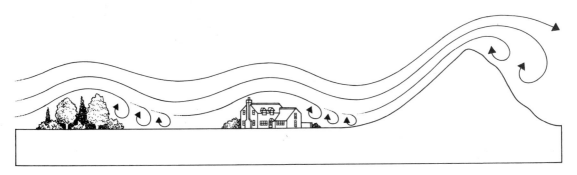

Fig 23 Turbulence close to the ground, and wind gradient

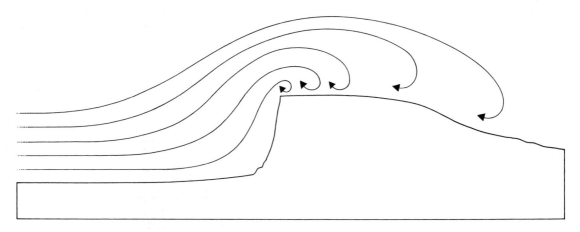

Fig 24 Lift and turbulence around a cliff

atmosphere will also, generally, cool with height, but not necessarily at the same rate as the thermal. The thermal will only exist as long as it is warmer than the air around it. Therefore, should the atmosphere cool quickly with height, the thermal will always be warmer than the surrounding air, so will keep rising. If there is no great temperature decrease in the atmosphere, the thermal will soon have cooled to be at the same temperature as the air around it, and will no longer rise.

The thermal consists of many thousands of cubic metres of air travelling upwards at as much as 1,000ft per minute, in the UK, and often 2,000ft per minute in other parts of the world. As this air goes up it will displace the air above it, which will drop down around the thermal. Where the two meet, there is often considerable turbulence.

Predicting Thermals

Predicting the presence of thermals is covered extensively later in the book, but as a basic guide, look at the following.

1. The history of the air. For this you need a good weather forecast, preferably one that shows a synoptic chart, with the pressure systems and isobars. If the air flowing over the country has recently been far to the north then it is likely to be pretty cold. If it has just wandered up from the south of France, it is likely to be rather warm. Therefore, a northerly component to the wind is likely if thermals are present.
2. The presence of thermals is often indicated by cumulus clouds, the fluffy, singular clouds that can often be seen during otherwise sunny days. These clouds are actually formed by the thermals; when the temperature inside the thermal has dropped enough, the water vapour that the thermal has carried from the ground will condense into water droplets and form cloud.

BASIC SKILLS

Launch

Paragliders are unique craft in that they have no 'primary rigid structure'. This means

Fig 25 Cumulus clouds marking thermals

that there is nothing keeping the wing in the correct shape except the fact that it is moving through the air, generating lift. This presents a particular problem on take-off. It is necessary to get the wing moving through the air in such a way that, as it starts to produce lift, it will be in the right place and at the right attitude. How this is achieved depends on the strength of the wind and, to a lesser extent, on the terrain at the take-off site.

Launch in Zero/Light Winds: The Forward Launch
When the winds are light you will have to run forwards during the take-off to generate sufficient speed for the wing to produce lift. Before starting, you should lie the glider out on the ground in an arc, as in Fig 27, so that it will inflate correctly. It is vital that the wing inflates at the centre first, and then at the tips. You must therefore ensure that the centre lines go tight first, and that the rest of the glider inflates symmetrically.

Once the glider is laid out, strap yourself into the harness, checking that everything is done up properly and is in the right place. Before you start to run, get hold of the A or front riser on each side in your hand, having made sure the rest of the risers go over your arm.

Go through your final pre-take-off checks, and check that your timing is correct, with regard to thermal cycles, and so on.

Run briskly forwards, keeping an eye over one shoulder to watch the wing inflate. As the tension comes on the lines, slow the run to give the wing a chance to catch up, but try to keep the pull even through the risers. Do not let your hand position effectively shorten the A risers more than is necessary to keep the glider coming up, otherwise the wing shape will be deformed and the glider may collapse.

Once the wing is overhead, release the A risers. The wing is now at the correct angle of attack, so extra pulling on the As will only deform its shape. Once you have

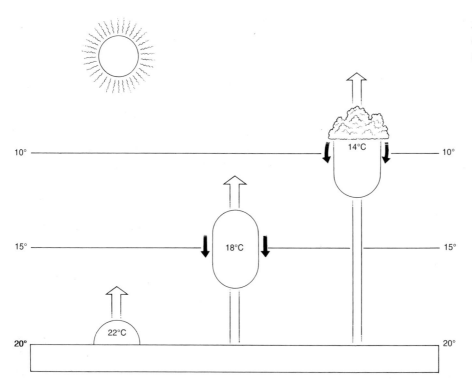

*Fig 26 Thermal
and associated
turbulance*

released the As, try to keep leaning well forward between the risers, with your hands held high to avoid pulling on any brake. Keep accelerating until the wing has lifted you into the air (*see* Fig 29).

Trouble-Shooting

1. If the wing stops half-way up, more pull is required on the A risers; just enough to keep the glider moving. Practice is required.
2. If the leading edge rolls underneath the wing, preventing air from getting in, there is too much pull on the As. If you find that the wing with less pull stops half-way up, try holding both the A and B risers when inflating.
3. If the tips inflate first, and the centre section collapses, the layout is too

straight; try pulling the tips further forward before inflation. This is a common problem on very high aspect ratio wings, some of which even have two A risers per side, so the pilot need only apply tension to the centre section of the wing.
4. If the wing inflates all right, but one tip is higher than the other, the layout is not straight. If there is room, try and angle your run towards the lower tip, and apply a little opposite brake. If it is too far off, start again from the beginning.

Launch in a Breeze: Reverse Launch
The stronger the wind, the easier it is to launch the glider, as the wing already has a certain amount of airspeed. Unfortunately, as the wind picks up, so the glider also seems to gain a mind of its own; it is therefore

Fig 27 Glider lying on the ground.

important to have some control over the wing at all times.

When there is an appreciable breeze, turn around towards the glider before you inflate it, so that your back is to the wind. When planning to do a reverse launch, it is a good idea to get into the harness and buckle up first, before stretching the wing out. In this way you are ready to control the wing as the air gets at it.

By pulling on various risers and brakes it is possible to get the wind to stretch the glider out into the correct shape for take-off. Generally, the rear risers (C or D) and the brakes will keep the glider down, while the A risers bring it up. The shape you want the glider to adopt is with the leading edge sitting up into the wind, with the remainder of the wing flat on the ground. This is called the 'wall', and is the essential first step to every reverse launch.

With the glider in a wall pointing forwards, and you pointing backwards, all the lines will be crossed over themselves. The way in which the lines are crossed will indicate which way it is necessary for you to turn as you take off. As long as everything is checked out correctly, and the wall is nicely symmetrical, then the glider can be inflated simply by leaning back against the wind, and pulling slightly on the A risers at the same time. Once the glider is above your head,

Fig 28 Canopy wall

25

Fig 29 (a) Take-off sequence

release the risers and turn around to face the wind. You are now ready to take off.

Trouble-Shooting: Building the Wall

1. If the glider rises off the ground, with the trailing edge first, reduce the pull on the rear risers and increase the tension on the As, so that the leading edge is in the airflow, but not enough that the leading edge comes too far off the ground.
2. If the glider is pulling too much, decrease the tension through the As by stepping back towards the wing, and pull more on the Cs or Ds. If the wing is being held down with the brakes or the D risers and is not settled, try holding it with the Cs.
3. If the glider appears to want to lift one tip first, the wall is not square into wind. Step back to increase the tension slightly, and

then step towards the side that is lifting. Manoeuvre side to side to ensure symmetry.

4. If the glider appears to want to lift both tips first, try and pull the tips down by pulling on the brakes, while still holding the glider down with the Cs. Ideally, the centre of the leading edge should be higher than the tips.
5. If the glider pulls you back up the hill, even holding the C risers, the wind is too strong to take off safely. Try pulling the whole glider down the hill a bit, but remember that although it might be safe to launch further down the slope, it is going to be tricky to top land, and the possibility of being blown back over the top of the hill will be greater.

Fig 29 (b) Take-off sequence

Fig 30 Reverse launch

Trouble-Shooting: When Inflating the Wing

1. If the glider comes up but carries on past you and collapses, too much tension is being pulled, either in all the risers together, or just in the As. As the wing starts to lift off the ground, just pull enough tension in the A risers to keep it moving. At the same time, you must walk up the hill underneath the wing, so that as it rises you move up the hill rather than the wing moving down it.
2. If the leading edge tucks under itself and stops the air from inflating the wing properly, there is too much pull on the A risers, and not enough tension on the rest. If, with a lighter pull on the As, the wing stops during inflation then try pulling on the As and the Bs together.
3. If the wing inflates but is off to one side, step quickly towards the lower wing tip – back underneath the centre of the wing – while the wing is still being pulled up. If the wing is established above your head and then goes off to one side, again step

underneath the centre, and also apply the brake on the opposite side.

PRE-FLIGHT AND PRE-TAKE-OFF CHECKS

There are three stages at which you should make a special effort to check your equipment and the prevailing conditions: as you unpack your gear, as you lay out or build the wall, and after inflation, before you leave the ground. There is nothing that does not need checking, on every flight, and it is a good idea to get into the habit of doing checks in a particular sequence.

Checks While You Unpack

As soon as you arrive at the hill you are going to be observing the activity going on. Are there other pilots there? Are they flying? Are they staying up? Are they having difficulty penetrating, circling in thermals, or

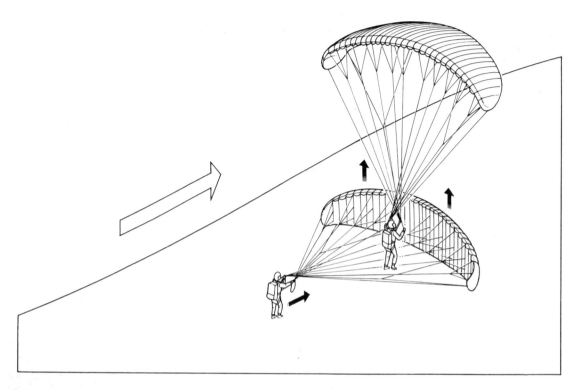

Fig 31 Reverse launch

scratching low down? Watching other pilots helps greatly, and talking to them is even better. It does not matter if you have never met any of them before; go up to them, introduce yourself and ask about the conditions. They are all there because they love flying, so you have something in common, and they are usually friendly. If there is nobody there, be very suspicious of the conditions and, even if things look good, do not fly on your own, unless you really do know better.

If you are at a site that you do not know very well, it is even more important to find out what you can from a local pilot. Not only are you interested in the conditions of the day but also the site rules (position of take-off, top and bottom landing, and so on), and also where the best lift might be found.

Once you have decided to fly, unpack your gear unhurriedly and examine it all as you take it out of the bag. Other than all the obvious things, also examine the reserve closure pin(s), if you have one fitted, the harness adjustment, and speed system operation.

Checks While Preparing

If the wind is very light, so that you have to lay out the canopy by hand, this gives you an ideal opportunity to check over both the top and bottom surfaces of the wing. This is easily done, but it can be very difficult to see small tears in the cloth so look very carefully. (I've spent half an hour looking for a rip that I knew was there.) Also, as you lay the lines out, have a good look up and down each one.

Line damage often takes the form of a broken outer sheathing that exposes the inner, load-bearing core to the elements. Fortunately, most manufacturers make the core and the sheath in different colours, so damage is easier to see. Broken lines should be obvious.

If the wind is stronger, these checks can be done as you build the wall. It is more difficult to see the top surface in this case, but much easier to see the bottom surface and the lines. If the sun is shining, rips in the top can be seen as light shows through on to the bottom surface; if the day is overcast and you are worried about the top surface, get another pilot to have a good look at it as you pull the glider up. Once the wall is built, all the lines are in clear view; it takes very little time to run your eyes up and down each one to check for damage.

In either case, once the glider is laid out check all the harness buckles and adjustments. The leg loops and chest strap should be secure, and the cross bracing, if fitted, adjusted to suit the conditions. Make sure that your helmet is on properly, and that all your ancillary equipment is ready: vario on, radio on, and gloves on).

Final Checks

Just before inflation, if you plan a forward launch, check the following: the risers are over your arms correctly; the sky ahead, above and behind is clear of other gliders; the weather is all right. If you plan a reverse launch, check your turn direction is correct; that the sky ahead, above and behind is clear of other gliders; that the weather is all right.

Do these checks after the glider is up, in the case of a reverse launch, or just before you run off, when forward launching. Look to see where all the other gliders are, especially any that are preparing to top land, who might need a bit of your airspace for overshooting. Check that your take-off is not going to force

any other pilot to alter his flight plan, and do a final check on the prevailing weather conditions. If all is OK, off you go.

IN FLIGHT

Once you are safely in the air you should be concerning yourself less with the canopy, and more with looking where you are going, and where you want to go. Most of the time when you are flying in the UK, there will probably be other pilots flying from the same hill, so it is essential that you keep a good look-out, and fly with regard to the basic anti-collision air law.

Fig 32 Flight planning – coastal ridge soaring

Flight Planning

At all times during the flight, you must have a flight plan that will involve not only what you hope to achieve in the flight but also how, at any particular time, you can get from where you are at present to a safe landing. If you are flying from a small hill in non-soarable conditions, you will already have checked, before take-off, that there is a safe landing area within an easy glide. Things become more complicated when the conditions allow you to gain height, and to soar away from your take-off area, either along the hill in ridge lift, or over the back when thermalling. The basic rule remains the same: you must, at all times and in all likely conditions, be able to fly from wherever you are to a safe landing area.

Your flight plan should also include some goal, or particular achievement, that you hope to attain during the flight. You should never take off with no particular aim in mind. During your early flying career, your task or objective might be just to soar and top land, but later on you will be looking to fly cross country, or at least to thermal away from the hill high enough to get away from the crowds.

Speed Control

Once you have taken off, and are safely away from the ground, the glider needs to be controlled for speed, as well as direction of flight. A paraglider will fly perfectly well at full speed with no pilot input, but this is not very efficient and it is better to fly with a little brake on at most times. When turning the glider, you should try to keep the speed as steady as possible; you do this by ensuring that the amount of brake applied to the inside is matched by the outside brake being

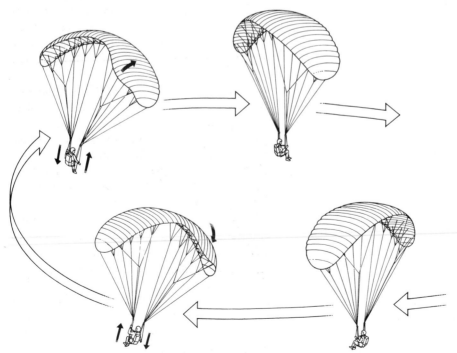

Fig 33 Neutal brake turn

released. It is also essential, when completing the turn, to apply the outside brake at the same time as releasing the inside one, all the time trying to maintain the same overall speed.

LANDING

Controlling Speed

The art of landing a paraglider is to arrive with as little ground speed as possible. There is normally some wind when you land, so the difference between your airspeed and ground speed must be accounted for. A general rule is that you must always land into the wind, although, because you are landing on your feet, it is possible to run off a certain amount of ground speed if things are not quite perfect. If things really have gone wrong, you use a parachute landing fall.

Because it is the ground speed, not the airspeed, that you hope to eliminate, the amount of flare (application of both brakes to slow the glider) necessary will depend on the amount of wind. In little or no wind, the glider will need to be flared completely, before touching the ground. If the wind is blowing at a speed in which the glider will happily fly, no flare is necessary, just enough brake to kill any forward motion.

Approach

Paraglider landings are described as top landings, side landings and bottom landings. These simply refer to the paraglider's location on the hill when it has landed. Each type of landing has its own special problems, techniques and each requires a different plan.

Generally, four different aspects of the landing need to be addressed on the approach:

1. you must land in an area clear of obstructions;
2. you must land into the wind;
3. you must have sufficient airspeed during the approach;
4. you must be flying in a straight line as you land.

Depending on whether you plan a top, side or bottom landing, you are able to ignore one of the above, but you must comply with the remaining three.

Bottom Landings

Both very inexperienced and very experienced pilots tend to do more bottom landings than pilots of moderate experience do. Once you have learnt to soar on a regular basis, all landing seem to be either top or side, until you have mastered cross-country flying, where you then land away from the hill, in what is effectively a bottom landing field.

Bottom landings often take place in very light wind, so it is possible to be fairly inaccurate with regard to landing directly into wind. Quite often the terrain will dictate the best direction in which to approach the landing, and a little running will compensate for any drift on touchdown. It is often gentler to land on a slight downhill, rather than directly into wind, remembering, of course, that the final glide will be that much longer.

Much more important is to make sure that you have plenty of airspeed during the approach. The more energy you have available when it is time to flare, the more effective the flare is going to be. Airspeed equals energy, so a nice fast approach followed by a well-timed full flare will reduce your ground speed almost to zero, even when there is no wind at all. Of course, if there is an appreciable breeze, the flare will need to be less emphatic; the aim is to achieve zero ground speed as you touch down. If the flare is too big, you will end up landing backwards and falling over.

As you are likely to need to do a fairly full flare to land satisfactorily, it is essential that you are travelling in a straight line (i.e. that the wing is level), as you flare. Any tilt will be amplified by the flare, and the glider will tend to swing violently unless you are able to compensate. Any compensation will lessen the effectiveness of the flare, so be ready to have to run a little.

Do not forget that not only do you have to choose an obstruction-free area in which to land, but that your glider will also need a clear area into which to fall once you have landed. If space is limited, as you touch down, keep running and ease off the brakes to give a little airspeed to the wing. This way you can keep the wing aloft long enough to guide it into a small area close by.

Top Landings

There are two major considerations that make top landings more complex. First, there is likely to be quite a lot of wind blowing, so the difference in ground speed with even

small changes of direction is quite great. Second, the top landing area is often quite restricted; not only is the gap between the lift zone at the front and the rotor area behind the hill small, but there are often a lot of obstructions on the hill top, including barbed-wire fences, parked gliders and parked cars. Good top landings always start out with a well thought-out approach.

Approaches
A top landing approach is either a crosswind tracking approach or a downwind leg approach. The crosswind tracking approach requires much less judgement, and also has the advantage that it can be aborted at any time; with the downwind leg approach, the pilot is committed straight away.

The crosswind tracking approach is more or less an extension of the normal soaring flight plan. If there is any side component to the wind hitting the hill, the approach starts at the downwind end of the beat. In any case, the turn at the end of the beat is maintained for longer than normal, so that you are now flying, crab-wise, back over the top of the hill.

As you approach the landing spot, turn into the wind, land, and collapse the glider.

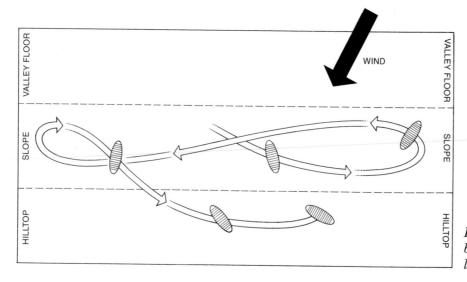

Fig 34 Cross wind braking, top landing approach

Fig 35 Down wind leg, top landing approach

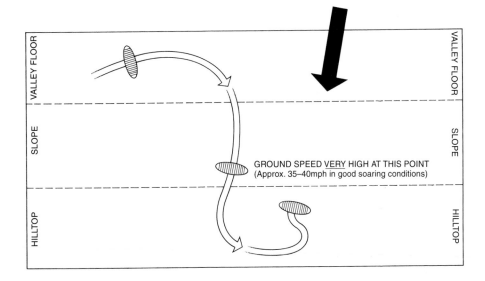

The figure labels read: VALLEY FLOOR, SLOPE, HILLTOP (on both left and right sides), and:

GROUND SPEED <u>VERY</u> HIGH AT THIS POINT
(Approx. 35–40mph in good soaring conditions)

Notice that at no time does the glider actually fly downwind; it is always facing slightly away from the hill.

The approach will need to be adjusted depending on whether you arrive high or low at the chosen landing spot. If there is a chance you will be low, it is important that you arrange things so that there is room to land short, if necessary. The only problem now is that you will be trying to land in the lift band, and you might find that as soon as you turn into wind the glider starts to lift. If this is the case then you will need to fly out and start all over again. If conditions are such that there is no more lift available, treat this landing as an across-slope, hillside landing (*see* page 34).

If you are too high as you approach, you have a number of options. At most sites it is safe to beat off the extra height behind the slope, above your chosen top landing spot. Be careful not to get too far back, because of the possible rotor, or too far forward, or you will just end up in the lift again. Another option is to pull the ears in to degrade the glide (*see* Big Ears', page 48) again, once you are over your chosen spot. The problem here is that you no longer have use of the brakes without the ears

popping out again. If the day is windy enough, though, this can be a good way of getting down. Be careful as you flare, because the ears will pop out just as you touch the ground. If you are too high, it is often best to fly out, away from the hill, lose height on the upwind side of the lift band, and have another go at the top landing from lower down. It requires good judgement, and it should be practised whenever you get the chance.

For the downwind leg approach, you fly straight towards the top of the hill, downwind, and turn through 180 degrees to end up over your chosen landing spot. The approach height is more critical than with the crosswind tracking approach, especially if there is a chance that you might end up low. The decision has to be made in plenty of time to abort, as this also requires a 180-degree turn. It is very dangerous to do sharp turns close to the ground, and considerable judgement is required to do a safe, successful downwind approach top landing.

Touchdown
The most critical component of a top landing is that you must be exactly into wind as you land. Small errors can be overcome by

differential braking, but landing well out of wind will cause you to be dragged across the hill, and into whatever objects are in the way. Landing while travelling in a straight line is not so critical, as the wing will still be flying above you as you land, so you will still have good control.

The fact that the wing is still generating lift is a feature of most top landings, and is also the cause of most of the problems. Many top landing sites are sloping slightly towards the front of the hill, and often, especially when the wind is reasonably brisk, there is considerable lift to be found, exactly in the area where you least need it. Unfortunately, there is no single, easy way to overcome this problem; the only answer requires considerable time practising both canopy control and approach planning.

Do not be tempted to fly in over your chosen top landing area and progressively pull on more brake to hover gently to the ground. Although this is a valid approach technique, it involves flying the glider into a wind gradient at slow speed, a manoeuvre that should be avoided by all the most experienced pilots.

Hillside or Cross Slope Landings

The ability to land on the side of the hill is one aspect of paragliding that really does set it apart from other forms of aviation. Because the wing is flexible, and a considerable distance away from the pilot, it is possible to arrange it so that it is still in clear air, and controllable, while the pilot is close to, and eventually standing on, the ground.

The basic technique behind a cross slope landing is to fly along the slope, not necessarily directly into wind, and to flare, while travelling in a straight line. If the wind is other than directly on to the slope, you need to be on the into-wind leg, and you need to be prepared to run a little, even doing a full flare.

Fig 36 Hillside landing, along the lines of solifluction

It is critically important that you are on the into-wind leg of your soaring beat when you attempt a cross slope landing, otherwise the speed can easily be too much, even for a good run. This means that you must start to think about your landing on the previous into-wind leg. If you do decide to turn downwind with the hope of finding more lift, you have to do two more 180-degree turns before you are next able to land. It is often better to land near the top of the hill after a shorter flight, than to do the extra turns and land half-way down.

Judgement is again important, but not as critical as when top landing. You must be travelling in a straight line as you flare, otherwise you will either turn into the hill, and land heavily, or turn away from it, and miss the hill at the same time as the glider stalls. If you are travelling along the hill and flare slightly too early then the wind will carry you into the hill, and you will still land successfully. If you are slightly late with the flare, you can normally run off the excess ground speed. A high flare when cross slope landing is often a very good idea.

It is possible to land when tracking slightly back towards the hill, but the timing of the flare quickly becomes critical. It is good to practise this, because it will enable you to land in small areas on hillsides, which takes considerable judgement.

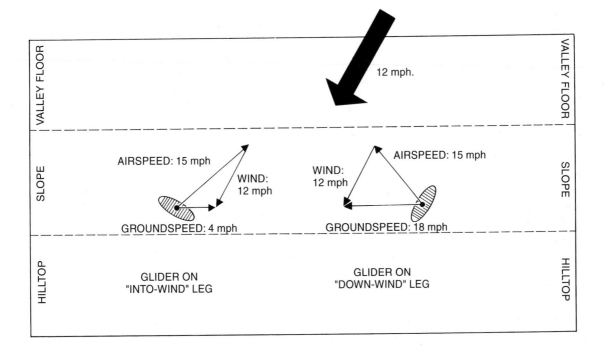

Fig 37 Ground speed on into- and down wind soaring beats

2 Intermediate Techniques

THEORETICAL AERODYNAMICS

The performance of a paraglider wing is related to the speed at which it is travelling through the air. As the speed of the air passing over the wing changes, so will the amount of lift the wing generates and the amount of drag. With an understanding of the changes in lift and drag, a theoretical model of the performance of the wing can be derived.

Angle of Attack

The primary control system of a paraglider consists of the brakes, which work as dragging flaps on the trailing edge of the wing. Other than speed systems and trimmers, these are the only available method of altering the angle of attack.

If both brakes are applied together, the drag generated by the trailing edge increases, the airspeed slows, and the angle of attack increases. The total lift will remain much the same, because the effect of the flaps on the trailing edge will increase the lift by a similar amount as the slower airspeed decreases it. The detail of what happens in this situation will depend on the design of the wing, and the trim speed that the manufacturer has set.

Drag

As the paraglider is primarily controlled by changing the amount of drag that the wing generates, a certain amount of complexity enters the equation. Theoretical drag is either 'parasitic' or 'induced'. Each type would normally change in a predictable way with changes in airspeed, but, as the primary control changes the parasitic drag, then its normal correlation to airspeed no longer applies.

Parasitic Drag
Parasitic drag consists of two elements – form drag and profile drag. Form drag is the drag generated by the air having to move around the solid objects (in the case of paragliding, the pilot, harness, lines and frontal area of the wing) that are travelling through the air. Profile drag is that which is created by friction on the surface area of the lift-generating wing.

Under normal circumstances, the parasitic drag will increase as the airspeed increases. This is exactly as you would

WING SECTION AT MAXIMUM SPEED.
– HIGH DRAG DUE TO HIGH SPEED

WING SECTION AT MINIMUM SPEED.
– HIGH DRAG DUE TO BRAKES

Fig 38 Aerofoil section, no brake and deep brake

expect, and also happens with cars, bicycles, and so on – as you go faster, the slowing force increases. The increase in the drag is in fact proportional to the square of the increase in airspeed; double the speed equals four times the drag. Against this, there is an increase in drag as the airspeed decreases, due to the increased amount of brake that the pilot must apply to slow down. Although this increase is somewhat outweighed by the drag increase with speed, it is still significant, especially when the pilot is attempting to fly at minimum drag (maximum glide) speed.

Induced Drag

Induced drag is the drag that is formed by the wing generating lift. As the wing passes through the air, the air pressure above the wing is decreased, while the pressure below is increased. Changing the pressure in the air requires some air to move, and thus drag is generated. Induced drag will also change with airspeed, although in the opposite sense to parasitic drag. As the airspeed of the wing increases, so the air will need to be moved less to generate the same amount of lift (there is more air passing over the wing per unit of time), and therefore less drag.

In actual flying, most of this drag is generated at the wing tips. The high-pressure air below the wing tends to migrate around the wing tip, thus creating tip vortices, and a certain amount of migration also takes place along the whole length of the trailing edge.

Total Drag

Total drag is simply the result of adding together the various different sorts of drag affecting the wing. The way in which the total drag changes with airspeed can be seen in Fig 40. At slow speeds, not much above the stall, the induced drag is most significant, the wing having to work really hard with the little bit of air travelling over it. As the speed is increased, so the total drag decreases, and everything starts to fly more efficiently. Unfortunately, it is not long before the parasitic drag becomes more significant, so the wing starts to lose efficiency due to travelling too fast. The speed at which to fly for maximum efficiency can be very precise, and will depend on whether you are attempting to fly to cover the greatest distance, or to stay in the air for the longest time.

Polar Curve

The polar curve is a graph of sink rate against airspeed, and is a useful performance

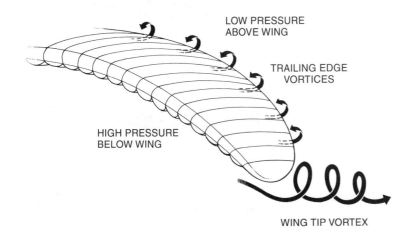

LOW PRESSURE ABOVE WING

TRAILING EDGE VORTICES

HIGH PRESSURE BELOW WING

WING TIP VORTEX

Fig 39 Induced drag turbulence

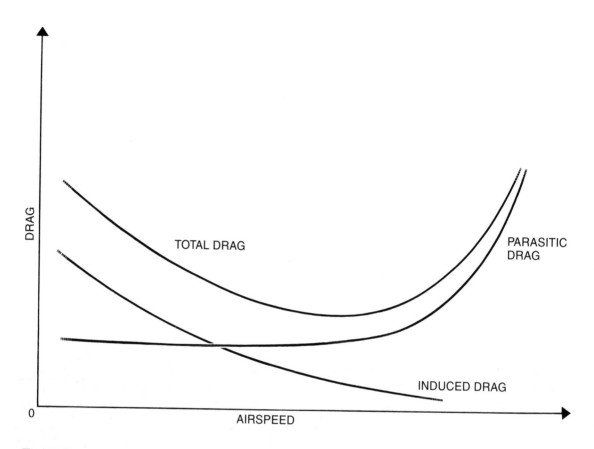

Fig 40 Parasitic induced and total drag curves

indicator for any glider. The ends of the graph will correspond to the minimum and maximum speeds of which the glider is capable, and it will also be possible to scale off the minimum sink speed and the maximum glide ratio.

Polar curves depend on many different factors. The lift the wing generates, and thus the sink rate, is directly proportional to the wing loading, so it can be affected by whether you are wearing lots of heavy clothes, or even whether he has had a big breakfast. The glide will also depend on the drag that you and the wing combination generate, so this will depend on whether you are wearing lots of loose clothing, or whether you are sitting up or supine.

Minimum Sink Speed

The minimum sink speed ('min sink') occurs where the value of the sink rate is at its lowest. This speed can be easily seen at the top of the curve in the graph. Under normal circumstances this is the slowest speed at which the glider should be flown. In the example in Fig 41, the glider's min sink is about 1.1m/s, and occurs at approximately 25 kph.

Maximum Glide Speed

The maximum glide speed ('max glide') is the speed at which the glider will cover the most

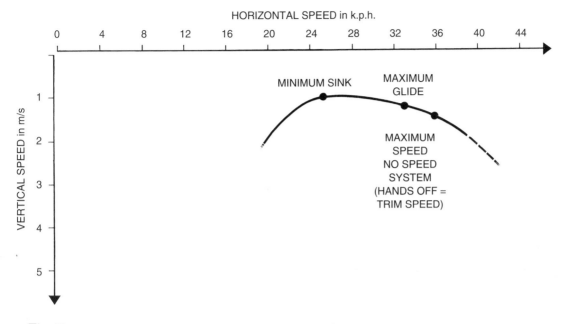

HORIZONTAL SPEED in k.p.h.

VERTICAL SPEED in m/s

MINIMUM SINK

MAXIMUM GLIDE

MAXIMUM SPEED
NO SPEED SYSTEM
(HANDS OFF = TRIM SPEED)

Fig 41

ground, in still air. It is measured by finding the tangent to the curve that passes through the origin. This value is of great use, as it is not such a natural speed to fly as min sink, but is the correct speed for the most efficient thermal transitions. The max glide for the example in Fig 41 occurs at approximately 33 kph, and it will be noticed that the sink rate at max glide is as much as 1.5m/s.

Speed to Fly

Theoretically, min sink and max glide are the slowest and fastest speeds at which the glider should be flown, assuming still air. If the glider is flying at a speed lower than min sink, it is sinking faster than it should, and going nowhere; if it is going faster than max glide, the glider will not get as far as it would if it had been flown a little more slowly.

It is very rare to go flying in completely still air. In the UK especially there always seems to be some air movement, either

Fig 42 Soaring over the English countryside

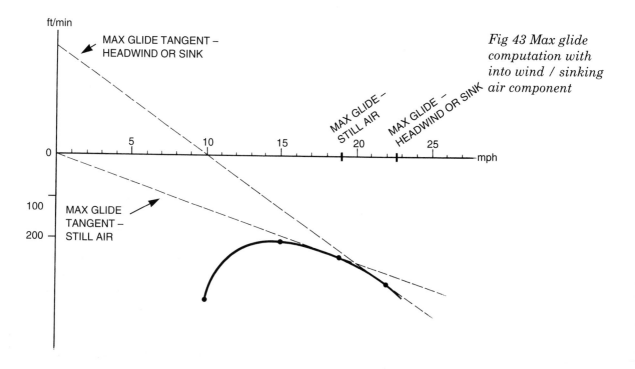

Fig 43 Max glide computation with into wind / sinking air component

horizontally or vertically, or more likely both; as soon as movement of any sort is introduced, the calculations (especially for max glide) become more complicated.

As we saw earlier, the max glide speed was calculated by taking the tangent from the origin on to the polar. To account for any air movement, either vertically or horizontally, we simply need to move the position for which we take the tangent.

Flying through sinking air is effectively the same as having a glider with a greater sink rate. Therefore, for the purposes of calculating the max glide tangent, we need to move the origin upwards by the sink speed of the air. As can be seen in Fig 43, the max glide very soon becomes the maximum speed of the glider. Flying in lift, the opposite effect is apparent; but if the glider is lifting then the max glide rate is infinite, so the best speed to fly is clearly one that keeps the glider in the lifting air the longest, and lifting the quickest ('min sink').

A head wind or tailwind has the effect of changing the speed that the glider is moving over the ground. Therefore, a head wind will move the origin to the right, and a tailwind will move it to the left. Flying into a head wind will very soon result in the max glide being the same as the maximum speed; and max glide being the same as min sink, when flying with a tailwind.

Trimmers or Speed Systems

Any trimmer or speed system will change the angle of attack of the wing, without changing the parasitic drag. The lift that the wing is generating will change, as will the induced drag. How these changes affect the wing will depend on how the manufacturer has set the glider up at its standard trim. Normally, the only positive effect is to increase the maximum speed of which the glider is capable, thus increasing its into-wind/through sink glide. Sometimes, though, it is necessary to use a little bit of

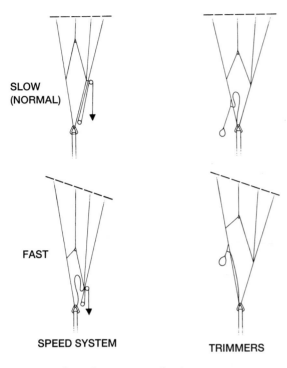

SLOW
(NORMAL)

FAST

SPEED SYSTEM

TRIMMERS

Fig 44 Speed system and trimmers

trimmer/speed system to achieve max glide speed. The glider's handbook should specify if this is the case.

To enable the trimmer or speed system to work correctly, the glider will need to have three or more risers, with some simple pulley system. When the system is applied, the effective length of the risers will be changed depending on their position. With a speed system (a pedal attached to the A riser), it is normal that the A and B risers are pulled down by the same amount, and the C riser by half this amount. The D riser stays the same length.

A trimmer (a cam buckle attached to the D riser) works in a similar manner, except it allows the D riser to become longer, as opposed to the A getting shorter.

Speed systems are generally more common on intermediate and advanced intermediate gliders; should they fail, this would happen in the slow (more stable) position. Trimmers are more common on Competition wings, as no effort is needed to keep them applied. Should a trimmer fail, however, the pilot will experience some quite severe problems.

Fig 45 Climbing towards cloudbase

GROUND HANDLING

With all ground handling, it is important to remember that there are no hard and fast techniques that guarantee success, but a few will guarantee failure. The whole procedure of building the wall, inflating the canopy and launching successfully is one where it is reasonably easy to achieve an acceptable result by many different techniques; if it works, it is the right thing to do.

For a successful launch, you must bear in mind the following objectives:

1. The wall must be even, with equal tension on both A risers.
2. The centre of the wing must be directly downwind of the pilot.
3. The wing tips must not be higher off the ground than the centre.

Although these objectives apply to any glider, they are especially important when launching a high-aspect ratio wing. It is possible to get away with all sorts of errors with training gliders that high aspect wings will not allow, when your technique must be nearer to perfect.

Building the Wall

While building the wall it is almost invariably easier to keep the brakes attached to the risers, and use the C risers to control the wing. Getting the wall even is reasonably straightforward, especially when there is a bit of wind blowing, but getting the wing tips to sit down can sometimes be a bit trying. The best technique I have found for this is to pull either the C, D or brake lines across, away from the tip, to pull more tension into the tip. Inspect the wing tips for asymmetry, as this is the best indicator of wind direction. If one tip is trying to lift before the other, you should move toward that tip. Also, if one tip appears to be being pushed in by the wind, and the other is not, again you should move in that direction.

Once the wall is built and even, you should be able to ease the tension in the risers let go of the Cs, and get hold of the brakes. If it is very windy on launch (say, more than 18mph), you will have to keep some tension on the C risers to keep the canopy under control; this can be reasonably easily done with one hand, whilst the other sorts the brakes.

LAUNCH

Launch Point Selection

Once the glider has been made ready for launch, it is quite easy to move it short distances to get into the best position for launching. This position is decided not only by obstructions, but also by the shape of the take-off slope, and the wind strength. As a general rule, the stronger the wind, the further down the slope you will need to be before you launch. This is because the glider wants to be in lifting air when inflated, in order to achieve a smooth take-off, and good penetration.

Pre-Flight Checks

During the wall-building procedure you will have been keeping an eye on the glider, lines, risers and harness, and will probably have noticed any problems. But it is important just before launching to have a good final look around, checking the equipment, weather and other pilots before continuing.

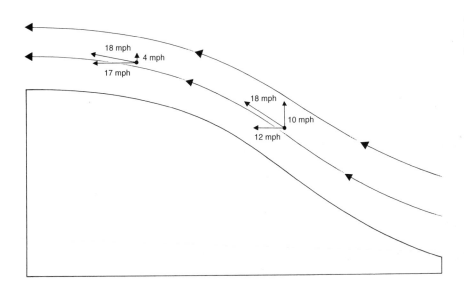

Fig 46 Horizontal component on hillside

Forward Launch

If there is no wind your wall building will have been done by hand. Make certain that the centre of the wing is going to inflate first. Everything else must be very neat, as there is no opportunity to sort out problems during the launch. With a little wind to help, things become much easier, but it is still important to ensure that the wing is laid out evenly.

You need to choose whether to 'snatch launch' (starting the launch run with all the lines between you and the wing loose, and snatching the glider off the ground), or 'tight-line launch' (with all the lines tight). The choice will depend on the wind strength (if any), and the launch site.

The Snatch Launch

Snatch launch if there is no wind, the launch site is reasonably open, and/or running speed is difficult (if, for example, there is deep snow on the ground). Make sure the lines are neat and that you are not going to run over any during the launch. If there is snow, stow the lines on top of the canopy material, not in the snow. This will prevent them freezing together.

As you start to run, accelerate as fast as you can, until the lines go tight. At this point you should slow your run, just make sure that you apply a good, steady pull to the risers. This way, the glider has a chance to fly over your head before you once again accelerate to take-off speed. Your running speed must be controlled by the pull felt from the risers, not the rate at which you are covering the ground. As you accelerate it is a good idea to apply a little brake, just to ease the glider off the ground and ensure that you are not caught out by any turbulence that might result in a tuck.

The Tight-Line Launch

You can use the tight-line launch if there is a little breeze, or the take-off is particularly steep. Having checked that the lines are free and you are ready to take off, merely step forward, applying tension to the front lines. Again, check the speed of your run. Let the glider come up above your head before accelerating and, as you pick up speed, apply brake as before.

Fig 47 Forward launch

Whichever technique you use, make sure you look up and check the glider before committing yourself to the air.

Reverse Brake Launch

The reverse brake technique has become the preferred technique when launching all wings, not just high aspect ratio wings. With this technique, each brake handle is held in the correct hand for looking forward, even when you have your back to the wind. This way, the brakes do not need to be released when you turn to face forward, so there is no time when the wing is uncontrolled. The disadvantage is, of course, that the controls are reversed while you are inflating the wing.

Once the wall is set up, the brakes should be removed and arranged so that the brake lines follow the crossed risers. The easiest way to achieve this, say, for a left turn, is to reach over the risers with the left hand, to grab the brake, and underneath with the right hand. This way you ensure that the brakes are twisted the same way as the risers.

Most pilots 'wear' the brake handles around their wrists when flying (so the fingers are not having to hold the brake handles, only rest on them). With this technique, as the brakes no longer need releasing during the launch, it is a good idea to slip the brakes over the wrists during set-up. This frees the fingers to pull the risers, and the brakes will fall to hand as soon as the canopy is up.

One word of warning: do not use the brakes in their crossed-over position to assist with the wall building on the ground. As you pull the brakes on, the lines will be wearing against the risers, and one side or the other will get weakened. Always use the risers to build the wall, and do not use the brakes until the glider is up above you. Even then it is best to have your arms slightly crossed to prevent any damage occurring.

Inflation

The modern trend among manufacturers is to build wings that require a constant light pull to inflate them. Gliders seem to be less prone to the dramatic overshoot that used to be common. It is essential, however, that you control the amount of energy that you impart

Fig 48 (a)
Reverse launch

to the wing during the launch. This is achieved by doing two things: first, walk up the hill under the wing as it inflates. This way, the glider is not travelling forward over the ground as it comes up (*see* Fig 31). This vastly reduces the amount of energy that the wing gains as it rises, therefore reducing the amount of brake necessary to stop the wing above your head.

The second thing you must do is walk sideways, if necessary, to ensure that the wing is centrally above your head as it rises. This reduces the amount of control input necessary to correct any error, although it does not alleviate the potential problem altogether.

Once the wing is overhead, and the risers released, it is likely that the brakes will need to be applied to hold the glider stationary.

Fig 48 (b)
Reverse launch

The amount of brake required will depend on three things: the strength of the wind, the steepness of the launch site, and the amount of energy imparted to the wing on inflation.

Just Before Take-Off

As soon as the glider is up, you should turn. There is little to be gained by remaining pointing up the hill, unless the wind is very strong and the glider is too far up the hill to take off on its own. In this case, you can walk the wing down the hill by leaning back more in the harness, thus putting more weight on the glider and increasing its airspeed. Ultimately it is easier to do this when pointing up the hill. As soon as possible, you should turn to face take-off direction. At this point you should hold the wing above your head with as little brake as possible just enough to prevent you moving down the hill.

Assuming the wing is stable and you are still on the ground, it is usually a good idea to stay in this position, standing on the hill, pointing forward with the wing flying above your head, looking around and taking note of what is happening in the sky. This ability to stand still with the wing flying is very useful, and should be practised until it is second nature. Not only does it give you the opportunity to do your pre-take-off checks, but it also gives you the time to look at what other pilots are doing, as well as feeling the air flowing over the canopy. It is easy to feel how 'lifty' the air is, simply by gauging the amount of brake necessary to prevent the glider moving forwards, and the pull of the risers.

Take-Off

As soon as you are ready, you need only raise the brakes a little, and lean forward between the risers to get forward speed on the canopy, and run gently off the hill. If the canopy is

Fig 49 Holding the glider overhead

deciding when you leave, not you, you have a lot of practice to do.

Launch Problems

The only problem that might occur just before take-off is small asymmetric tucks, caused by turbulence, by another glider flying in front, or (more likely) by letting the glider overtake slightly. The wing will tend to tuck more easily because it is lightly loaded, and therefore has less internal pressure. Small' asymmetric tucks are those that are recoverable without the wing collapsing, and the whole procedure having to be restarted.

The technique to be used in the case of

small tucks is as follows. The first and most important thing is to keep the wing square above your head. In order to do this, you must look at it. (This is the opposite of what you should do if the tucks happened in the air, where it is important to keep looking along the intended flight path.) Probably a little opposite brake will be required, although often the most important first stage is to load the wing up slightly, by walking forward, or squatting down in the harness.

Do not, at this stage, be tempted to pump the deflated side vigorously, as this will just collapse the canopy. The best course of action, once the wing has been accelerated a little, is to apply even brake on both sides. This will often clear the tuck, without allowing the wing to yaw, which would probably cause a tuck on the opposite wing. It is vital that the yaw is controlled rather than the tuck – most tucks will clear themselves eventually, and if you are on the ground there is no need to worry about time.

HANDLING IN THE AIR

Active Flying

The term 'active flying' is used for all times when the glider is being piloted, rather than when the pilot is behaving just as a passenger. It does not mean that the pilot is making control inputs all the time, just that you are ready and able to make a control input should the circumstances demand.

The basics of active flying are twofold. First, you should be concentrating on keeping the paraglider wing stable and centrally above your head. This means that you should counteract any movements that the wing should make due to turbulence. Second, you should be controlling your speed, and, to a lesser extent, direction of flight, with respect to the flying conditions.

Maintaining Angle of Attack

The paraglider wing will have a pre-set trim angle of attack; the pilot has limited control over this with any trimmer or speed system that is fitted, but the trim angle is basically set by the line lengths. At the same time, because of the large gap between the centre of pressure and the centre of gravity, it is common for turbulence to disturb the trim angle by a noticeable degree. If the turbulence is strong enough, it is possible that it will be able to displace the wing sufficiently for the angle of attack across part of the leading edge to become negative, thus causing the wing to tuck. It is most likely that this displacement will be in both pitch and yaw, which is why asymmetric tucks are more common than symmetrical ones.

Maintaining a positive angle of attack is simply a case of reacting quickly with the brakes to any displacement that you notice. If you feel the wing start to accelerate, you must apply brake to check it, and as the wing drops back you must release brake to accelerate it. This way you will be able to keep the glider centrally above your head, always with a positive angle of attack.

As well as reducing the risk of the wing tucking, flying actively will also increase the efficiency of the wing. If the angle of attack can be kept reasonably constant, both the lift and the drag generated will also be constant, and the wing will perform better. If you can smooth out the bumps, you will be flying the wing at its best.

Speed Control

The greatest effect the pilot can have on the angle of attack is, of course, by operating both brakes together, thus changing the airspeed. Maintaining a positive angle of attack can be achieved by flying at a reasonably slow speed. Care should be exercised, however; if you fly too slowly, the angle of attack variations due to turbulence could result in stalling. As a general rule, it is better to fly as close to the centre of the speed range as possible.

Of course, in some situations this might not be possible. The worst case is where the turbulence is associated with strong winds, and you are needing to fly fast just to maintain your position over the ground. There are three possible courses of action in this situation, as follows.

1. Rather than fly at mid-speed, let the glider fly faster, but always maintain positive brake pressure. By doing this you will be able to feel what is happening to the wing, and will still have a little brake range left to damp out the oscillations.
2. If this is still not fast enough, start to use the speed system cautiously. Push gently so that the wing is not displaced any more than is necessary. If the wing is already oscillating in pitch slightly, wait until it is at the forward end of its swing before applying the stirrup. This reduces the change in angle of attack; the wing is already at a low angle of attack, and as this angle increases so the speed system will work to keep the wing central above you. It is important that during this time you maintain positive brake pressure. Do not use the trimmers to increase your forward speed in this situation, unless you really do have no alternative.
3. If things still look bad, try pulling the ears in, and applying full speed system. Having the ears in will not make the glider go any faster, but it will increase the internal pressure in the wing and greatly reduce the risk of the tips tucking. Be careful, though, if the situation you find yourself in requires you to land in this configuration, say, at the top of the hill. As you touch the ground, the canopy will quickly become unweighted (your descent rate will be relatively high), and is likely to collapse initially and then re-inflate very quickly. The best way to avoid the

resulting drag back is to prepare to collapse the wing as you hit the ground with the A risers, as they are already in your hands, and try and catch the wreckage. This technique of using the speed system with the ears in is very useful when you are landing in the mountains, in a strong and turbulent valley wind. The decision to land is normally made at 1,000ft at least, and it is common to see pilots approach from this height with 'big ears'.

RAPID DESCENT TECHNIQUES

Big Ears

'Big ears' is a technique of collapsing the outer cells of the wing, providing an

Fig 50 'Big ears'

increased sink rate and greater stability. The technique is to reach up and pull down the outer A lines, far enough to get a negative angle of attack on the leading edge. The affected area of the wing will then fold back beneath itself and, on some gliders, will stay in that position with no further pilot input.

How many lines to pull depends on the total number of lines. The maximum would probably be half the available lines on each side (for example, if the glider has four lines on each side, you pull down two).

B Line Stall

A B line stall is a very effective way of losing height quickly, but it takes the glider out of its stable flight envelope, and requires both room and correct technique if you are to

Fig 51 B line stall

recover from it safely. A B line stall should only be used when you need considerable height loss, for example, when escaping from a too-active cloud. You should never need to B line below 500ft; it certainly takes at least 200ft to recover.

The B lining technique is to reach up to the top of the B riser with both hands and pull the risers down evenly. The initial resistance is quite significant, so it feels more like picking yourself up. The glider will feel as though it is slowing (which it is) and dropping back behind you, and is similar to, but not as dramatic as, entering a full stall. As you keep pulling down, you will settle back below the wing and start to sink quickly. It is necessary to pull the B risers down by at least 6 inches to get the wing to stall properly, and you can increase your sink rate by increasing the amount you pull.

The technique for recovery is simply to let the B risers out, back to their normal position. There are two things to remember here:

1. it is imperative that the risers are released quickly, so that the glider tends to rock forwards and regain airspeed;
2. the risers must be released symmetrically, so that the glider recovers in a straight line.

There are a couple of points to note about a B line stall. The glider's forward speed is greatly reduced while B stalling, so if there is a noticeable wind you should expect to drift as you plummet. Also, different wings react in different ways when B stalled; some descend in a stable attitude, some thrash about wildly. However the glider reacts when stalled, it is important that, on recovery, you check that the glider has regained forward speed, and is not stuck in a stable deep stall. If the glider is still in deep stall – and you will know because you will still be sinking fast – recovery is best done by either pushing forward on the A risers, or giving the speed system a good kick. You are effectively trying to rock the glider forwards. You can also recover from a deep stall by applying the brakes, either one or both, which has the effect of rocking the glider backwards.

TUCKS AND CRAVATS

Asymmetric Tucks

Minor Tucks
An asymmetric tuck occurs when the angle of attack on one part of the wing becomes negative. Minor tucks, affecting perhaps just a few cells toward the wing tip, are quite common, especially in thermic conditions. More major ones, affecting around 40 per cent of the wing area, say, are much more rare, and normally the result of a combination of circumstances, one of which is often pilot error.

Minor tucks often occur when one wing tip exits the core of a strong thermal, while the majority of the glider is still in it. As the glider is still lifting, the outer tip has a negative angle of attack, and will tuck. This is often compounded by the pilot, who has real-ized that he is flying near the edge of the core, and therefore tightens his turn by reducing the amount of outside brake. The resulting tuck is invariably small, because if the majority of the wing exits the thermal core, the whole glider will dive away from the thermal, and will probably stay fully inflated.

More Major Tucks
For more major tucks to occur, the glider will normally need to have been displaced in yaw as well as in pitch. How this actually occurs is dependent on the circumstances, but it should fall into one of two groups. Either the glider has been flown fast through turbulence, or it is the process of recovery from some radical manoeuvre. The effect, though, is much the same. The wing tip folds back, and underneath the glider, all the A lines go loose on one side, and the pilot falls to one side of the harness, and swings away from the tucked side.

This swinging action is the cause of the greatest problems. If unchecked, the swing of the pilot will put a considerable roll input into the wing, and start the spiral. As the glider spirals, the speed will increase, and so will the internal pressure. This will have the

Fig 52 Asymmetric tuck

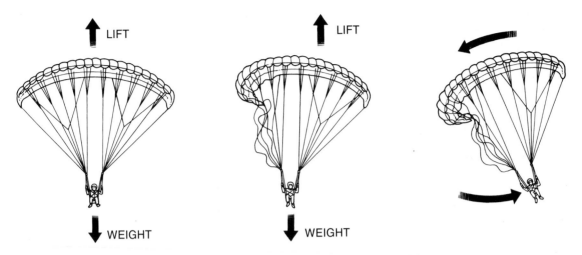

Fig 53 Asymmetric collapse

effect of clearing some of the tuck, but leaving the glider spiralling, and descending quite quickly.

The speed at which all this happens will depend both on the type of glider and on the reason for the tuck in the first place. A stable intermediate will almost certainly recover more quickly, and with less turning, than a Competition wing. But, do not be lulled into a false sense of security. If you are in rough air, even the most benign training canopy can spiral well following an unchecked asymmetric closure.

It is worth noting here that Standard Class wings are not only likely to recover more quickly than Performance and Competition wings, but also to be more stable in yaw. In rough conditions, the glider is less likely to suffer a really big tuck, and therefore less likely to spiral. But, especially when recovering from a well-established amplitude maximum spin, any glider is likely to yaw to quite a considerable degree. *See* 'Cravats', page 53, for more details on exiting spins.

Asymmetric Tuck Recovery
There is a general procedure for recovery from an asymmetric closure that should be followed in all cases when you know or suspect that you have suffered a tuck. You should not look up at your wing to see whether or not you have a tuck; not yet, anyway. In the case of a very large tuck, there are a few further techniques, but the more normal procedure is as follows.

1. Maintain a safe flight path through the air. Look in the direction in which you want to be going, and make sure you are actually heading that way. Do not expect to have to apply full opposite brake if you have a small tuck on an intermediate, but be ready to react very quickly if you get a large one on a Competition wing close to the ground. If the tuck occurs while thermalling, and the glider is not immediately turned away from the lift, carry on circling and sort the tuck out later. It is best if you tighten the turn slightly away from the tuck, towards the thermal core, so you can then fly straight for a while as you pump the tuck out.
2. Pump out the remains of the deflation. Now is the time to glance quickly up at the wing to check if it is still tucked, how much pumping will be required, and if

51

there is anything more serious happening. The pumping action needs to be long and positive, not quick little pushes. Some wings, especially Performance ones, might need a couple of good heaves on the brake to get the final cells re-inflated. As long as most of the wing is flying and you have directional control, there is no urgency to clear it in one go. Most Standard Class wings will re-inflate themselves very quickly while you are still concentrating on maintaining a safe course, but you should still have a quick look to check.

3. Re-establish the wing in a stable position above your head. How much the wing is displaced from its normal trim position will depend on both what you have had to do to recover, and also the speed at which the wing is re-inflated. A Standard Class wing is liable to re-inflate more quickly, but more dramatically than a Performance wing, and is therefore liable to need more input to re-establish stable flight.

The situation can be different if you have suffered a really big asymmetric tuck, probably on a Performance or Competition wing. In this case, not only will the remains of the wing be off to one side of you, thus making straight flight impossible initially, but the amount of brake required to re-establish straight flight with the small amount of remaining wing might stall it. Should this happen, you would end up spinning in the opposite direction to the initial spiral; this might be fun over water with a rescue boat, but of limited entertainment value at your local hill.

Recovery in this case depends on the height that you have in hand. If you have sufficient height to let the glider turn, then this is the first thing to do. As the glider starts to turn, so the energy builds up quickly. Use this energy to help both pump out the deflation and turn the glider back onto its original course. Full opposite weight shift as the glider swings will achieve most of the desired effect, plus a little opposite brake once the speed has built up.

If there is insufficient height to let the wing spiral, concentrate on missing the ground and forget the asymmetric tuck altogether. If you are flying on the hill, and can miss the ground by whatever means, do so. After landing, you need to analyse why you let yourself get into the position where you suffered a big asymmetric close to the ground. Big asymmetrics should always be avoidable. If you are not able to miss the ground, you will be in a lot of trouble.

Symmetric Tucks

Occurrence

Symmetric tucks are less common and easier to deal with than asymmetrics. They can, however, look more dramatic, as the whole of the wing often collapses, rather than just a tip. For a symmetric tuck to occur, the centre section of the wing, at least, must have a negative angle of attack. Many of the Standard Class wings now available have a degree of wash-in (an increased angle of attack towards the tips) built in, which reduces the severity of symmetric tucks, but it is certainly possible to get a more or less complete collapse on any glider. This is because, as soon as the centre section collapses, the increased drag in the middle tends to push the tips forwards, thus decreasing their angle of attack, and increasing the tuck.

Symmetric tucks will only occur at high speeds, so avoiding these is the obvious way of avoiding tucks. If full speed is essential, be ready for the wing to go in the centre, by keeping in touch with the wing through the brakes.

Recovery

As with asymmetrics, if you think the wing has tucked, first maintain course, then apply brake to both sides, which will invariably re-inflate the wing, and then re-establish stable flight. Only then can you, carefully, increase the wing back to full speed (assuming this is still necessary).

It is possible to induce a symmetric tuck by being over-enthusiastic when pulling in the ears. In this case, release the outer A lines, apply brakes to re-establish stability, and try again; this time, be much more gentle.

As with asymmetrics, it is possible to suffer a significant symmetric tuck when exiting from a radical manoeuvre. If the exit occurs in a straight line (more likely from a full stall, say, than from a spin), the resulting dive might cause the centre of the wing to go. If this happens, simply applying both brakes will recover the glider. It should be possible to avoid this situation completely, by suitable training on performing stalls and active flying or, better still, by avoiding stalling altogether.

Cravats

Occurrence

A cravat is where one wing tip becomes caught up in the remaining lines. A cravat is normally stable that is, it will not recover itself but is normally easily recovered, as long as you have some height to play with.

Cravats are very rare under normal flying, especially on a Standard Class glider. To get a cravat, the glider has to yaw to an extreme degree, and it is normally only on recovery from some unstable manoeuvre, a spin or possibly a stall, that such yawing occurs.

Recovery

To recover from a cravat, you must first make two decisions. First, is the paraglider still pilotable? (In other words, can you still

steer?). Second, do you have sufficient height to follow the recovery procedure?

If you can steer, and there is not a great deal of height remaining, it is probably better to land the glider with the cravat still in, being aware of the increased sink rate.

If there is plenty of height, the best recovery procedure is to pull in a big asymmetric tuck on the cravat side, and hope that recovery from this will clear it. This often works but, even if it does not, it is worth noting that a glider with a big asymmetric is more likely to be pilotable than one with a big cravat. Another option is to full-stall the glider, reducing the wing to an unstable mess, and recover from that. Experience of full-stall recoveries is recommended before you attempt this course of action.

If the wing is totally unpilotable, and spiralling, the full-stall recovery is the only option. Be prepared to deploy your reserve if you are in this situation.

A big cravat close to the ground is easily avoidable. If you do find yourself in this situation, however, prepare for a heavy landing. Remember again that a wing with an asymmetric is more controllable than one with a cravat, but, in either circumstance, expect a high descent rate.

PILOT-INDUCED UNSTABLE MANOEUVRES

Full Stalls

Aerodynamically, a full stall is where the angle of attack of the wing is too great for the air to flow smoothly across it.

When the wing is stalled, there is no lift developed by the aerofoil, but plenty of drag. This drag tends to reduce the forward speed of the glider to near zero, but the lack of lift will increase the vertical speed very quickly. As the airspeed is increased, so the wing will resume normal flight.

With most aircraft, where the angle of attack can be altered without directly affecting the airspeed, it is possible to stall the wing at a speed greater than the minimum speed of the wing. With a paraglider this is not the case. The only way the angle of attack can be altered far enough to stall the wing is with the brakes. These will directly affect the airspeed, so in effect the paraglider will only stall at minimum speed.

To enter a full stall you need do no more than apply both brakes fully. On many wings you will also need to take one, or perhaps, two wraps of the brakes to get the wing to stall cleanly. As the wing slows the inertia that the pilot has will in itself add to the increase in angle of attack, until the wing is behind you, and virtually stationary.

As the wing stalls, you will feel a sensation similar to falling backwards off a chair. At this point, with the wing well behind the pilot, it is important that you do not release the brakes. (If you were to do this with the canopy far behind you, it would probably overshoot so fast that you would end up falling into the wing.) You must wait until the glider, despite being totally collapsed, is either above or, preferably, slightly in front of you. At this point you should release the brakes to about shoulder level, thus enabling the glider to regain flying speed. The glider is still likely to overshoot by a fair amount, so you must be ready to re-apply the brakes to regain stable flight, and clear any tucks.

Parachutal or Deep Stalls

The parachutal stall, or deep stall, is very different from the full stall. When a paraglider has gone parachutal the wing is still inflated in much the same way as in normal flight, but the airflow is no longer over the wing from front to back; it is now more from below to above.

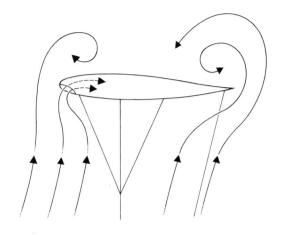

Fig 54 Aerofoil in deep stall

In a parachutal stall there is still a certain amount of low pressure generated above the wing, by the air rotoring around the leading and trailing edges. The direction of travel of the glider is, more or less, vertically downwards, at a fast sink rate, but far from dropping. There is sufficient air travelling past the cell openings at the leading edge, and sufficient low pressure above the wing to keep the wing inflated. From the pilot's point of view, the situation looks pretty normal.

How to Do It

To get a glider into a parachutal stall it is necessary to slow the wing to below stall speed, but without deforming the wing shape by applying the brakes. There are two ways of doing this, either of which might result in a parachutal stall.

The first, most common way is by performing a B line stall. During a B line the forward speed of the wing is reduced to near zero, but the wing is kept in reasonable shape by the airflow over the rear section. If the B line is exited with extreme care, by gently releasing the B risers, the wing can be returned to normal shape without any increase in airspeed. The wing is then in a parachutal stall. (This is why you are always advised to release a B line quickly.)

The second way of entering a parachutal stall is by slowing the wing down by using the risers or speed system. It is not easy but it is possible with some gliders.

Recovery

However the stall is entered, recovery is the same. Assuming the glider is stable in a parachutal stall, it is actually only statically stable, not dynamically (in other words, if it is displaced, there is no force trying to return the glider into its stable state). Therefore, to recover, all you have to do is displace the glider, either in pitch or roll. Assuming sufficient height, the best course of action is to try to rock the glider forward, either by operating the speed system or pulling on the A risers. Other options include rocking the glider backwards by pumping the brakes (but this tends to lead to quite a big dive), or trying to turn the glider with the brakes (but you must take care not to spin the glider).

However the recovery is instigated, the glider is bound to dive forwards as it regains forward speed, so you must be prepared to react to this.

Notes

1. Recovery from B line, both slow and fast, is now included within the Certificate of Airworthiness, to check for parachutal recovery. Very few modern gliders will stay in a parachutal stall for more than a couple of seconds.
2. It is possible with some modern, high-performance wings that the glider will enter a parachutal stall if the brakes are applied when the trimmer or speed system is set on full fast. This should be avoided.

Spins

Aerodynamically, a spin is where one side of the wing is stalled, while the other side is still flying. The stalled half tends to stand still, while the flying side turns quickly around it. If the spin is allowed to develop, both you and the glider will rotate about a central axis, fast but not necessarily at the same rate.

To enter a spin it is necessary for the glider to be flying slowly, near to its stall speed. In this situation, if one side is allowed to accelerate quickly, or the other side is slowed dramatically, it is likely that the glider will spin. If you combine these two manoeuvres, the wing will spin very quickly. Unfortunately, it is quite common to be flying slowly, circling in a thermal, so you must always be aware of the possibility of entering an unintentional spin. This is especially true if the sky is crowded with other gliders, and the possibility of having to make a sharp turn to avoid a mid-air collision is correspondingly greater.

Two Types of Spin

There are two types of spin that can be entered intentionally. The simple form of the spin is called the 'flat' spin. This is entered by flying the glider at close to minimum speed, and then simply applying one brake fully. This is a simulation of the sort of spin you may have if you try too hard in a small, punchy thermal. Initially, the glider will feel as if it is lurching to one side (the slow side), and if the slow brake is raised even slightly at this point the glider will regain normal flight. If the brake is held down, you will feel a rearward acceleration as the wing starts to spin, but the glider will stay approximately above your head.

The second spin type is called the 'amplitude maximum' spin, in which one of the pilot's hands is fully down, the other fully up during the manoeuvre. 'Amp max' spins are entered in a similar way to flat spins, except that as the glider starts to lurch, the slow hand is held down, and the fast hand let completely off. This is more like the sort of spin you might get yourself into if you are thermalling slowly and suddenly find another glider in the way. As such, it comes under the heading of easily avoidable problems. The speed of rotation in an amp max spin is extremely fast; often the glider rotates faster than you do and the risers can get twisted up very quickly.

Recovery
The initial recovery procedure from any sort of spin is the same. The slow wing needs to be speeded up, simply by releasing the inside brake. Vigorous opposite brake, to halt the rotation, should be avoided, as this tends simply to reverse the direction of the spin, without letting the glider accelerate.

Although the glider will now be flying properly, it might still have a certain amount of rotational energy; the actual amount will depend on the severity of the spin. As the glider regains speed, it will dive forwards, and it is likely to suffer an asymmetric tuck, on the opposite side to the spin direction. If the spin is severe enough, the possibility of getting a cravat is correspondingly greater. Whichever is the case, follow the procedures outlined in the previous sections to recover the situation.

Twisted Risers
If the risers become twisted, either at the start of the spin, or on recovery, a number of alternative techniques are available, depending on the severity of the twist.

If there is a single twist, or the twisting motion has stopped, it might be possible to reach above the twists, grab the lines or risers and twist the harness back again. Alternatively, again if the twist is not too bad, try pulling the risers apart at the bottom.

If the situation is more serious, and the

glider is still spinning, the best bet is to try and reach the B lines, and B line stall the glider. This will stop the spin, and give you time to untwist. This will require some altitude, so make sure you have plenty to spare. It is generally not a good idea to full-stall the glider in this circumstance, as the brake lines tend to get trapped in the twisted risers; the glider will remain fully stalled until all the twists are out, and the recovery is both delayed, and uncontrolled.

If none of the above is possible, or there is a chance of running out of height before a full recovery is made, the only remaining option is to pull the reserve parachute. If you are still spinning, the reserve will open extremely quickly and stop the spin instantaneously.

SPIRAL DIVES

Spiral dives should not be confused with spins; aerodynamically they are totally different, and they are not really unstable manoeuvres. During a spiral dive the glider is progressively turned sharper and sharper until the pilot (and the C of G) is rotating about the wing (and the C of P).

During a well-established spiral, the rate of descent of a Standard wing can be greater even than when B line stalling; so the spiral is a good fast descent technique. Some say it is fun, but some find it makes them feel very ill.

Entering a Spiral

To enter a spiral, it is necessary to turn the glider reasonably quickly, although be careful not to overdo it and enter a spin. As the turn gets established, keep applying the inside brake, and also weight shifting towards the turn. As the centre of the glider

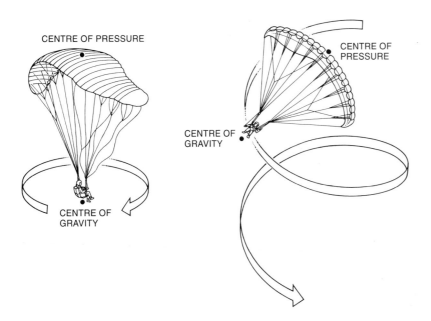

Fig 55 Spin and spiral dive

CENTRE OF PRESSURE

CENTRE OF PRESSURE

CENTRE OF GRAVITY

CENTRE OF GRAVITY

gets closer to the horizon you will feel the G forces increase and also an apparent acceleration. Very soon you will feel as though you are hanging out horizontally from the wing, and spinning around it very quickly.

Depending on the glider, you will either need to maintain inside brake or weight shift (or both, or, in a few cases, neither) to keep the glider spiralling. A steady descent rate of greater than 2,000ft per minute is possible if a good spiral is maintained, and it is also possible to get the pilot (but not the glider) travelling in excess of 60 mph.

Recovery

Recovery from a spiral dive is very simple, but does take some time, and therefore height. The glider should be steered straight in a gentle fashion, so that the wing stops descending, but is initially still turning. This will probably require some outside brake to be applied, along with opposite weight shift. The idea is that the glider loses all the excess speed while still turning, rather than diving

out of the spiral and subsequently climbing uncontrollably. If you do let the glider climb too quickly, expect the glider to feel as though it first stops, then dives forwards and probably gets a large asymmetric tuck. Recover as described above.

Because of the speed that it is possible to attain in a spiral, there is considerable extra stress on the glider, and lines. In a straightforward spiral this is within the safety limits, but be careful not to increase the stress by pulling in the ears while spiralling. As, when in big ears, you are effectively reducing the number of A lines by half, it is quite easy to get too close to the limits of the glider's structural integrity, and you risk a complete line failure.

THE PARAGLIDER HARNESS

Adjustment

Proper harness adjustment is very important, not only for comfort while flying, but also for the feel of the glider, which

Fig 56 Weight-shift turning

is affected by the harness, and the stability.

Proper harness adjustment should allow the pilot to do the following when on the ground:

1. stand up straight;
2. be able to walk around easily;
3. look upwards and see all parts of the wing.

Proper harness adjustment should allow the pilot to do the following during take-off:

1. lean through the risers to accelerate;
2. adopt whichever position he likes upright or supine;
3. sit back without having to use the hands.

Proper harness adjustment should do the following during flight:

1. allow the pilot to move between upright and supine;
2. prevent the shoulder straps falling off the pilot's shoulders when upright;
3. allow the pilot to find the speed system with ease;
4. give sufficient support to the pilot's legs.

Proper harness adjustment should, during approach, allow the pilot to stay upright, without holding the risers.

If your harness does not allow sufficient adjustment, or has the wrong geometry, to enable you to achieve all of the above, you will need to have some major adjustments done professionally, or purchase a new harness. It is vital that the harness allows enough freedom of movement to enable you to sit upright and prepare to do a plf easily.

Sitting Back after Take-Off

This used to cause some of the worst problems during take-off, but now is almost cured, with the advancements in harness design as well as pilot education. The problem is that, as your feet leave the ground, you are stranded, hanging in the leg loops, without being able to sit back comfortably. The old cure for this used to be to let go of the brakes and shuffle into the harness, holding the sides. Letting go of the brakes just after take-off is very bad practice, especially if the

Fig 57 Paragliding harness

conditions are anything but totally smooth.

If your harness does not let you sit back easily without using your hands, hold both brakes in one hand while you use the other to manoeuvre into the harness.

Whether you find it easy or difficult to get into the harness, it is important to wait until you are well clear of the ground, and have checked that the glider is flying properly, before you do so. If things go wrong at this stage, it is imperative that your feet are down and ready to run or do a plf, so that you do not end up on your back.

Cross-Bracing

Most modern harnesses have, or have the facility to have added, adjustable cross-bracing. Although it means two more buckles to use every time you take the harness off or on, this is an extremely useful feature; it not only makes the glider more stable in rough air, but makes the ride more pleasant for the pilot in the same conditions.

Adjustments to the Cross-Bracing
Unlike the fixed cross-bracing available on some older harnesses, adjustable bracing has a gradual effect depending on how loose or tight you set them. At full loose, the harness will behave as if there is no cross-bracing at all, allowing maximum weight shift but also maximum instability. Ultimately though, even loose cross-bracing will help a little if something really dramatic were to happen, like a bigger than 75 per cent tuck. Full loose cross-bracing is really only for amazingly smooth evening floats, or for smooth coastal cliff flying.

Tightening up the cross-bracing a little will not have much effect on the normal flying characteristics, but the glider will feel slightly more roll stable in big weight-shift turns. At full weight-shift you are pushing against the cross-bracing, so there is some force trying to return you to neutral. In turbulence there will also be some smoothing out, but no appreciable loss of feel. This setting would be appropriate in 'normal' conditions.

With the cross-bracing adjusted to around two-thirds of its tightness, the glider will tend to feel quite heavy to weight shift, and thus start to feel a little uncoordinated, but much more stable, especially in roll, in rough conditions. Tight thermalling is more difficult, but much less effort is necessary to keep the wing centralized. This is a good adjustment when you are expecting 'active' flying, immediately after take-off.

With the cross-bracing fully tightened (with no tension through the chest strap), the glider will feel much more solid, and the brakes will feel less responsive, as there is no weight shift available to help turning. Equally, the glider will tend to fly better through bad turbulence, as there is no possibility of the weight being shifted against the turn. Tight thermalling can be tricky, and the possibility of entering an unintentional spin will be increased, because all the turning has to be done with the brakes. If you feel you need full cross-bracing before you take off, you may need to question your decision to fly at all.

How to Adjust the Cross-Bracing
It should be possible to adjust the cross-bracing with reasonable ease in the air, even in quite turbulent conditions. Remember that tight cross-bracing can be achieved either by tightening the actual cross-brace straps or by loosening the chest strap. Two techniques are useful here; there are probably others, and you need to experiment. Especially if the conditions are getting rough, you must avoid releasing one or both brakes.

The first technique often used is to hold both brakes in one hand, and reach down with the other. In this way the pilot is able to keep in touch with the wing through the brakes, but has the disadvantage that steering is impossible until the operation is complete.

The second technique is used when the pilot has the brake handles around his wrists when flying. He simply lets the brake ride up his arm while reaching down and adjusting the cross-bracing. A degree of caution is needed in this situation to avoid flying too slowly, but it is possible.

Other Harness Designs

Totally Open Harness
This harness has no cross-bracing, and just a single chest strap. It is probably not to be recommended for use with any but the most stable of beginner wings, or in coastal conditions. It can easily be modified to accept adjustable cross-bracing, but this is only worth doing if the harness is comfortable enough. Many of these harnesses are of an old design and not very user-friendly.

Fixed Cross-Braced Harness
This harness often has no chest strap, just a pair of cross straps. It is very stable but will make even quite a lively wing feel dead in the air, and this type is therefore often used in schools. Again, they are often of an old design, uncomfortable, and difficult to modify.

Semi Cross-Braced Harness
This is a harness where the hang points are well outboard of the shoulder straps, and arranged in such a way that the single chest strap can be tightened to provide some cross-bracing. Most modern harnesses are of this design, even those that have the option of adjustable cross straps. You should bear two things in mind when using a harness with semi cross-bracing. First, they are often difficult to adjust in the air, especially loosening, where they tend to go totally slack. Second, as the cross-bracing is tightened, so the hang points move closer together. The problem here is that the closer the hang points, the more likely it is that the risers will get twisted if the glider spins.

Speed System Stirrups

Most gliders now need a speed system for their best performance, so it is normal to have a stirrup fitted. Although easy to use, and tucked well out of the way while flying, it can be awkward when ground handling and manoeuvring on the ground. Also, it can sometimes be difficult to find in the air; often, the pilot needs to take one hand off the brakes to locate it.

Most harnesses now have some sort of stirrup stowage device fitted, either in the form of Velcro or elastic straps, which can be used to hold the stirrup clear of the ground. This works well enough, but a hand is needed to release it before the stirrup can be used. If you think that extra speed might be required soon after take-off, either due to wind speed or performance considerations, it is important to release the speed system before you leave the ground.

To help locate the stirrup in the air, you could try using a length of 'bungee' cord tied to the stirrup at one end, with a loop in the other to slip over one foot. It is important to get the length right, so that it does not go totally tight when the glider is flying and the pilot's feet are down, but is still long enough to hold the stirrup when the leg is extended in flight. It is even possible to put one foot in the stirrup soon after take-off to help you get back into the harness; this should be done very cautiously.

3 Thermalling

PREDICTING THERMALS – THEORETICAL

Lapse Rate

Lapse rate is the predicted rate at which the temperature drops with altitude. Generally, the lower atmosphere (from the surface up to the tropopause) will get colder the higher you go, although the exact amount by which it gets colder will depend on the prevailing weather conditions. This is known as the Environmental Lapse Rate. The air contained within a thermal will also get colder as the thermal rises, due to the reduction in pressure with height. This is known as the Adiabatic Lapse Rate (adiabatic cooling is cooling due to reducing pressure). If the environmental lapse rate is greater than the adiabatic lapse rate, then the atmosphere is said to be unstable, and thermal conditions will exist. If, on the other hand, the environmental lapse rate is small (that is, it's almost as warm at altitude as it is on the surface), then the atmosphere is stable, and there is little chance of any thermic activity.

The exact adiabatic lapse rate will depend on the amount of moisture in the air as well as the temperature. Dry air will cool at approximately 3°C per thousand feet (this is the dry adiabatic lapse rate, or DALR), whilst saturated air (such as that inside a cloud) is closer to 1.5°C per thousand feet (SALR). Thermal air, on its way to cloudbase, will cool at approximately the DALR, so, if you can predict that the environmental lapse rate is going to be greater than this, thermals should be expected. Refer to Fig 26, on page 24.

Fig 58 Waiting with patience

PREDICTING THERMALS – PRACTICAL

From the Ground

If the wind is too light to soar easily, you will need to predict the presence of a thermal while you are still on the ground. This is not as difficult as you may think.

Climbing out away from the hill when there is apparently no wind blowing is very satisfying, especially if all your friends are still on the ground wondering how you knew that the thermal was there. There are a number of clues that will give away the presence of lift; watch for these and be ready at all times.

Clue one is the presence of things such as seeds, bugs, butterflies, and so on being lifted in the air just in front of take-off. Clue two is things eating clue one. You will often see swallows, swifts, and other birds circling around in the rising air, grabbing a quick bite on the wing. Clue three is the thermal affecting trees, crops, and so on, just in front of the hill. Often, the rustling of leaves on the trees at the base of the hill will be enough of a clue to encourage you to take to the air.

The final and most useful clue is the wind strength and direction at take-off. As the thermal approaches, the air rising in front of the hill will tend to pull the wind (if any) off the hill. The next bit of air movement up the hill should, in theory, be thermic air, so you want to take off as soon as possible. If there really is no wind blowing at all, you might need to do a nil wind launch as soon as the tailwind stops.

If there is some wind, but not enough to soar, lifting air can be detected by the behaviour of the glider above your head. To do this you will have to master the art of standing on the hill, in light wind, with the glider flying above you. Practise this until you can do it without having to think about it.

As well as finding it more difficult to keep

Fig 59 Climbing away

the glider up as the wind drops with the approach of the thermal, you will also notice the glider pulling forwards, as the angle of attack of the wing increases. This increased angle of attack is due to the airflow over the wing going from near horizontal, in the normal wind, to more vertical, in the thermic air. This effect is much more noticeable than you may think; a reasonable thermal just in front of you might require full brake just to stop the wing from pulling you off the hill. Still, if there is a good thermal there, taking off is just what you want, so let the brakes up a little, give a good push and you should be away.

Another interesting effect, due to the same bit of physics, is that it appears to be a lot easier to inflate the glider in thermic air than in normal circumstances. Be immediately suspicious if you pick the glider up and it appears to be much keener to over-fly you than normal. (This is not to be used as an excuse for poor ground handling.)

From the Air

If there is a soarable breeze, the situation suddenly becomes much easier. With a bit of luck there should now be a wide scattering of thermal indicators spaced evenly along the hill – other paragliders. Do not just rush into the air, however, unless it is one of those rare days when it appears to be lifting every-where. Take a few minutes to look at the other paragliders and try and work out where the thermals are the best, how often they are coming through, and how well the other gliders are doing in them. If you can take off straight into a thermal, you will immediately gain height over the other pilots, and be in a better position to make the correct decisions regarding getting away or not. Generally, it is much more difficult to gain height than it is to lose it, so the higher you stay the better.

If the wind is quite strong and forward progress difficult, you might have no alterna-tive than to take off in the lighter conditions just before the thermal comes through. Hopefully, you will be able to use this lift at least to get forward of the hill-top and thus into easier conditions, if not up and away and gone. Be very circumspect in these conditions, though; one misjudgement will see you over the back of the hill with little chance of getting forward again; only attempt this if circum-stances allow for landing behind the top.

THERMALLING TECHNIQUE

First Thermal from the Hill

The basic rule of thermalling is that you must follow a flight path that keeps you in the rising air. As the thermal is initially rising up the front of the hill, this means staying in one area of the slope, probably doing reasonably tight S-shaped turns. However, soon the thermal will have lifted off the top of the hill and will start to be carried downwind by the general air movement (if there is any). When flying within the thermal, you really need to be doing consecutive 360-degree turns.

The point at which you stop S-turning and start to 360 will depend on the strength both of the thermal and of the wind carrying it. Generally speaking, you should attempt to start circling as soon as it is safe to do so; the lighter the wind or stronger the thermal, the sooner this will be.

If there is virtually no drift, you can take off, fly out in the lift and start to circle straight away. Be warned: in these circumstances the other paragliders that you left on the hill will take off behind you as soon as they see you going up. They will be in the way and stop you circling. This is bad etiquette on their behalf – it loses the thermal for all of you (no one can turn because of paragliders on every side of them) – and the pilots responsible should be made aware of their mistake. Do not do this yourself.

A stronger thermal will allow you to do tighter 360s; you can start earlier than you can with the big, wide circles that are neces-sary with weak lift. Stronger wind will have the opposite effect; an early 360 could easily take you back into the compression and a top landing instead of climbing out.

While close to the ground, the thermal will normally be leaning over slightly, in a down-wind direction. As you are dropping down through the thermal (at your normal sink rate), you will need to adjust your position slightly after each 360 to stay in the rising air.

After your first circle, fly back into wind for a few seconds before turning again. This should keep you reasonably centred within the best part of the thermal, and climbing well. If you have done a series of 360s and lost the lift, it is usually because you have fallen out of the downwind side of the thermal, so it is best to search initially back upwind. This is a good idea anyway, as it will take you back towards the hill, and the best area to look for the next thermal.

Take-off scene during a busy competition.

Gliding to the next thermal.

Ridge soaring, waiting for a thermal to come through.

Starting the first climb to cloudbase.

Coastal soaring o the cliffs in the Is of Wight.

A fully equipped pilot taking off at the beginning of a competition task.

Coastal soaring with friends.

A 'gaggle' of paragliders thermalling at the beginning of an XC flight.

The UP Vision, a modern intermediate paraglider, just after taking off.

Cross-country flying in the Lake District.

Fancy dress at the St Hilaire festival in France

Waiting on a take-off ramp for the next thermal.

Thermalling over the English countryside.

*Pilot and passenger enjoying
a tandem flight.*

A pilot checking his wing prior to taking off.

Scratching' – flying low in the ridge lift.

Preparing to top land above a coastal cliff.

An Edel high aspect ratio paraglider over the Lake District.

Gliding off in the search for more lift.

*Gliding towards the
sunshine and,
hopefully, the
next thermal.*

*Tandem team
thermalling to
cloudbase.*

Once you have gained a couple of hundred feet above the hill you should start to map out the thermal. Increase the size of your 360s to search for areas of better lift. If you fly into some stronger lift you should fly straight for a few seconds then continue to circle. If you fly out of the lift while circling, do not be tempted to turn back the other way. It is much more efficient to continue in the same direction and to straighten up after 270 degrees to fly back into the core. Note that this is not the same as hitting a thermal which pushes you out of it when you are looking for your next thermal while gliding (*see* page 68). Again, fly straight for a few seconds on re-entering the lift before continuing to circle.

Other pilots will provide a great deal of useful information. For example, if you are climbing steadily and you see another pilot climbing at about the same rate 100 metres away, it is fair to assume that the area of lift you are in is quite large and that benefit may be gained from flying flatter, more efficient 360s. It is also worth searching the sky between yourself and the other pilot, as you may both be climbing in weaker lift with a better core between you.

Once you have found a good core you should concentrate on spending the maximum amount of time in the strongest area of lift. Many pilots do not fly tightly banked 360s but try to fly the apparently more efficient flat 360s. If there is a better core, a tightly banked 360 may increase your sink rate by 100ft per minute, but may enable you to stay in lift that is 300 or 400ft per minute faster than the surrounding air. Watch the better pilots at your local sites and you will see how they out-climb other pilots by really working the best lift. Just how aggressively you should be turning is proportional to the strength of the thermals. Treat the gentle days gently, but do not be afraid to attack the stronger days a little more.

At some point during the climb you will need to decide whether to commit yourself to this climb, or to abandon it and head back to the hill. Sometimes this decision will be easy, as you will be able to gain a couple of thousand feet without drifting out of gliding range of the hill. On light wind days this will be reasonably common, and you may even reach cloudbase directly above the hill. On stronger wind days you will need to make an earlier decision.

Some pilots try to maximize the distance they can drift back in lift by pushing as far forward as they possibly can. This works quite well, provided that the air is buoyant on the day in question – the pilot will, in effect, be making a series of small climbs and upwind glides. On days when the thermals are strong but widely spaced, a pilot flying further out from the hill may find that the approach of a thermal reduces the wind speed, and that the lift band no longer reaches out to where he is flying. He may be in the thermal earlier than those pilots closer to the ridge, but they are likely to be rather lower down at the same time.

On days such as this, any thermal big enough to be worth committing to will almost certainly be drifting slowly enough for you to climb high enough to decide to stay or go before you have drifted very far over the back of the hill. Big thermals contain a large mass of air that has been almost at rest on the ground, and it takes a little while for the wind to build up the momentum of such a large mass. In other words, the good climbs that are likely to take you all the way to cloudbase on moderate to strong wind days will be drifting much more slowly than you might expect. It is not uncommon for a good thermal to haul those pilots who are airborne off on the start of a good cross-country flight only for it to become too windy to take off for some time, as the thermal increases the wind on the hill after it passes through.

The problem on the light wind days of having to wait until you are clear of the hill before being able to 360 will not normally apply on stronger days; the ridge lift will keep pilots high enough to 360 pretty much as soon as the thermal is entered. The trick is to fly straight out from the hill for as long as possible before starting to turn, but without flying out of the thermal. This is not at all easy when flying on your own, but becomes much easier if there is someone upwind of you – just be prepared to turn as soon as they start sinking, provided it is safe to do so, of course. Keep checking where other pilots behind you are, and do not forget that they will be converging on the thermal from both sides. Of course, if you fly into a good strong core, you should start to turn in it after the standard three seconds, rather than continuing upwind regardless. If you fly into good lift which fails to last more than a couple of seconds of straight flying, quite often you will encounter a short section of sink before hitting another larger, stronger core.

Subsequent Thermals

The first thermal is always the most difficult, not least because of the proximity of the hill from which you have launched. Subsequent thermals are normally a more predictable shape and also, with a bit of luck and forward planning, you should reach subsequent thermals when still at least a thousand feet or so clear of the ground. This also applies to the initial, climb-out, thermal when you have launched from a winch.

As long as your prediction has been successful, you should be able to fly into the thermal reasonably close to its centre. It is unlikely that you will notice much roll movement of the glider, certainly not as much as you would on a hang glider or sailplane, but you will notice an apparent speeding up of the wing as the angle of attack adjusts itself to the rising air. As you catch this by applying brake, your vario should start to beep nicely. At this point you have to make the decision about which way to circle. Factors that will affect this decision include any other gliders already in the thermal (circle in the same direction), any feeling of being turned by the thermal (circle against the turn), and your own circling preference.

Assuming that you are not so close to the ground that any lift at all is essential, you can afford to start searching out the core of the thermal straight away. As you circle, try to build up an imaginary, three-dimensional picture of the thermal; work out where the better bits of lift seem to be, and also the edges. The two techniques that will enable you to do this quickest are the same as when coring the thermal away from the hill. First, as the lift increases, decrease your turn (best done by reducing, or even reversing, the weight shift); and second, extend your 360s in various directions to see how the lift changes. This way, you can plot out the best bits and centre on them.

Fig 60 Gliding to a good source of lift

4 Cross-Country Flying in the UK

METEOROLOGY

Meteorology is a huge and complicated subject on which many comprehensive books have been written. (*See* Further Reading for recommendations.) We have not entered into similar detail here, but the following is a selection of meteorological tips that may prove useful.

Ideal Cross-Country Conditions

In Theory

In order to fly the greatest possible distance cross country, you need the weather to co-operate with you. In order to determine what features to look out for from weather forecasts, let us design our ideal cross-country day in the UK:

1. we want good strong thermals, to make the climbs easy and quick;
2. we want a high cloudbase to give us the maximum glide distance and search time for the next thermal;
3. we want a comparatively strong wind for maximum drift (for distance), or very light winds (for triangles, or out and return flights);
4. we want to ensure that the clouds are not going to over-develop or form showers.

For good strong thermals, we need a cold airmass with the minimum of cloud and haze

to ensure that plenty of sunshine reaches the ground to heat it up. The airmass behind a cold front will be cooler and clearer than the warm wet air in a warm sector, so post-cold-frontal conditions are going to be better than warm sector or pre-warm-frontal conditions. (Good wave conditions can often be found

Fig 61 Classic XC conditions in the Lake District

ahead of an approaching warm front, so do not give up altogether.)

Of greater significance is where the airmass originated and what it passed over on its way to your favourite flying site. As we are hypothesizing about the ideal day, the airmass flowing over the country will have originated in the Arctic. This means it will be cold, which in turn means that it will be unable to carry much moisture. This in turn will lead to a high cloudbase and also very clear air. The lack of industry in the Arctic means that we are also benefiting from fewer smoke and dust particles in the air; hence, haze is at a minimum. In order to prevent any clouds that do form at the top of our designer thermals from over-developing, we would want a high inversion to prevent runaway development without killing all thermal activity, so we will need to be on the edge of a high-pressure system.

Do these kind of conditions exist, and what should we look for in the TV weather forecasts in order to predict them?

In Practice

The ideal weather pattern does appear every now and again in the UK, and occurs as follows. In order to get cold clear air down from the Arctic, there must be a stable pattern of high- and low-pressure systems. The Azores high will occasionally extend in a huge ridge up to the east of Iceland. This will pull the airmass from the Arctic down over Scandinavia and across the North Sea to Scotland. This is a reasonably short sea crossing and the water is relatively cold, so only a little moisture will be picked up by the air during the crossing. A low-pressure system in the vicinity of Germany is then useful to pull the airflow round from the north-east to a north or north-westerly flow, ensuring that it flows over as much of the UK as possible. Big distances can be flown on days with weather patterns such as these.

Airmass Types

This 'ideal' airmass is known as the Arctic Maritime airmass, and represents the best conditions for excellent flying. It is a cold airmass warmed from underneath, making it unstable, but dry enough to ensure there will be no over-development.

There are five further airmass types, each of which offer different flying conditions. These are as follows (in a clockwise fashion).

The Polar Continental airmass originates in the polar regions of northern Europe and Russia. In the winter and spring months the air will be as cold and dry as for the Arctic Maritime airmass, will pass over the land-mass of Europe (hence 'Continental'), and will remain mainly dry. Any moisture picked up from the North Sea will usually fall as snow on the eastern coastal regions. Some smoke and dust will be picked up as the airmass passes over the industrialized areas of northern Europe, so the quality is not as good as that of the Arctic Maritime air. The sun will not be high enough over the winter to create any useful thermal activity, but there is potential for good conditions as the days lengthen in early spring. In summer, this airmass will arrive as a warm body of air with much haze from the smoke of Europe's industry reducing the heating effect of the sun.

The Tropical Continental airmass originates in the north of Africa and arrives in the UK having passed mainly over land. It is not noted for providing particularly good flying, with the thermals tending towards the 'bullet' variety, which can be unpleasant to fly in. This is also the airmass from which summer thunderstorms are normally experienced. If you fly on a Tropical Continental day and clouds start to form, keep a careful eye on their development.

The Tropical Maritime airmass originates over the sea near the Azores. It passes over water all the way until it reaches the UK, so it is not surprising that a good deal of cloud and rain is expected from it. In summer there is a chance of it providing good conditions away from the coast.

The Returning Polar Maritime air originates in the polar regions but travels a great distance over the sea before approaching the UK from the south-west, and will thus have lost the benefit of starting as a cold dry body of air. It makes for relatively poor flying conditions.

The final type is the Polar Maritime airmass, which offers the likelihood of some good conditions again. The air will have originated in the same region as the Returning Polar Maritime airmass, but follows a much shorter (and colder) path over the sea before reaching the UK; it is correspondingly cooler and drier. The air will not have passed any industry on the way, and the resultant clarity will help the generation of good thermals. This is a more commonly occurring airmass than the Arctic Maritime, and will provide the majority of the good flying days each year.

Sources of Information

The weather forecasts from the BBC are a good source of information, including synoptic charts and overnight low and daytime high temperature forecasts. Video the forecasts so that you can pause the recording to study the synoptic charts and wind strengths. Try to relate the wind strength that you experience on the hill to the spacing of the isobars on the charts and you should be able to judge the strengths more accurately than the forecast. The television forecast has two advantages: first, it provides a look ahead over several days (or, in the case of the farming forecast on BBC1 on Sunday lunch-times, a whole week), and second, it is readily accessible to just about everybody.

Note that similar isobar spacing around high- and low-pressure systems represents markedly different wind strengths: the wind around a high-pressure system is stronger than would be expected for the same spacing around a low-pressure system.

A second source of information which you may find useful is the MetFax service, which provides detailed synoptic charts for noon (GMT) today and + 24 hours. For this you need to have access to a fax machine or a fax modem on a computer.

The third source is AirMet, a telephone message forecast aimed directly at pilots. This provides a great deal of information about the location and progress of weather fronts, wind strengths and directions and air temperatures at various altitudes, and also the freezing level and warnings of hill fog or turbulence. This is very useful information that will enable you to determine the degree of stability of the day (the lapse rate), and the likelihood of the clouds forming showers. The disadvantage of this level of detail is that the forecast covers only a twelve-hour block. It is good for checking on the morning you intend to fly, but not much use for planning where to go if you need to travel far to get to a good site.

Many pilots consult a combination of the above sources, as well as Internet weather pages, when deciding where to fly.

OBSERVATION OF CONDITIONS

Before Arriving at the Site

Observing the conditions to gauge the type of day begins even before you get to the site. If the cumulus are popping at 8 o'clock in the morning, you can expect the sky to over-develop pretty quickly. I normally drive past several flags to get to my favourite flying area, and these are a very reliable indicator of whether it is blown out on the hill before I am less than half-way there. I normally carry on to the site anyway, just in case, but it is seldom worth the effort!

Before Take-Off

The sky is clear and blue, the air is cool and crisp, and the flags are signalling 'Go' as you arrive at the site. Keep observing. Is anybody else flying yet? If nobody else is there, are you at the right site? If others are flying, what does the air look like? Is it worth hurrying to launch? Is one part of the ridge working better than another? Keep watching while you are preparing your glider. Prepare yourself for the flight by putting on your flying suit, map case and so on. Telling yourself you will land and kit up properly when conditions start to improve means that you are guaranteed to miss the first good thermals of the day, and they may prove to be the last. When you judge conditions to be right (probably before anyone actually leaves the hill), take a leak and then take to the air. It is difficult to concentrate on flying properly with a full bladder, and it will be cold at cloudbase.

RIDGE SOARING

You watched where the others were getting the best lift while you were getting ready, now you should try to work out what is working, and exploit it. Check not only the ground sources but also the clouds forming within flyable range of the ridge. Are you getting better results from the ground sources or the clouds? This information will be of greater importance to you later in the flight when you need to find another thermal and do not have the ridge to fall back on. Are the thermals big and soft, or small and angry? Modify your style to fit the conditions. Fly gently on the gentle days, but do not be afraid

Fig 62 Ridge soaring, waiting for the first thermal

to put in some really sharp turns if the sky is more boisterous.

Some pilots venture as far out from the ridge as possible, to provide the maximum distance to drift back in while thermalling before having to commit to leaving the hill. This seems a good idea in theory, but practical experience suggests that, as the wind drops as a thermal approaches, this will reduce the ridge lift, causing the pilot to sink out just before the thermal arrives. If a thermal is good enough for a climb-out, it will almost certainly provide a good enough climb to drift ratio to give you the confidence you need to commit to the climb. If there is a thermal trigger in front of the hill, it may well be worth pushing out this far. The thermals will be breaking away before reaching the main slope, but this is the only circumstance in which this will be worth trying.

CLIMB-OUT

Once you start to climb out, you cannot afford to relax your vigilance. You will gain more valuable information about the way that the thermal strength varies with altitude. Does an initially strong climb peter out to almost nothing long before base? Or does a weak thermal become a screamer above 3,000 feet? This too will affect your decisions throughout the rest of the flight, so the better you observe the conditions now, the easier your decision-making will be later in the day.

Once you are established in your climb, take a look at the clouds downwind at regular intervals to decide which are growing and which are decaying, and how long they last.

AIR LAW

The basic avoidance rules are covered in Appendix 1 on air law. What will concern you once you are away from the hill or winch site is the airspace. Below are some pointers to what you can and cannot fly through, and how far you should stay away from restricted airspace.

Airspace

There are a few hard and fast rules governing airspace, but also a number of grey areas.

You may not fly in an ATZ without permission from the relevant air traffic controller. You may be able to fly over the top of the ATZ, that is 2,000ft above the marked runway height, which is shown beside the runway on the airmap. You will need to be very confident that, if you lose your thermal, you will still be able to glide clear even in sink; allow a couple of thousand feet clearance before venturing over ATZs. It is usually easier just to fly around them, but there are some areas where two or three ATZs are located side by

Fig 63 Starting to climb out

side. In this case, try to fly across the overlap to reduce the distance needed to glide clear.

The rules governing MATZs are not quite so clear-cut. You are allowed to fly through a MATZ (but not its enclosed ATZ) unless prevented by local by-laws, or unless you ask for and are denied permission by air traffic control. Given this situation, it is clearly advantageous not to ask for permission from air traffic control in those situations where a by-law is not in place. Your decision whether or not to fly through a MATZ should be based entirely on safety grounds. Many RAF bases that operate fast jets will be quieter at weekends than during the week, and midweek flying around such bases is probably to be avoided. You cannot rely on being spotted by fast jet pilots. If all is quiet, you may proceed with caution through a MATZ.

Danger Areas are similar to MATZs. Some

are always active, others only at certain times, and they vary both in area and height. Some may be only 500ft high, while others extend up into space and may be used for testing missiles. Similar to Danger Areas are Restricted Areas, from which you may or may not be excluded. The only way to sort out which affect you is to spend time studying your airmaps. Each of the Danger Areas and Restricted Areas on the airmap has a number. The key at the bottom of the airmap has details concerning these areas; do not throw this bit away when you cut your map up to make it easier to carry in your map case.

Airspace Classes

There are seven classes of airspace in the UK, which are designated by the letters A to G.

Class A airspace is off limits to paragliders, as they cannot comply with the requirements which must be met to fly in this airspace.

Class B airspace covers the entire country above FL245 and is therefore not relevant to paragliders. (If you do find yourself approaching 24,500ft in the UK, you should probably consider setting off on a glide!)

Class C airspace does not currently exist in the UK.

Class D airspace changed status during March 1997. Prior to this date paragliders were allowed to fly in certain class D airspace without the need for air traffic control permission. Permission is now required for *all* flights into Class D airspace. It may be sought by contacting the controller via the appropriate radio channel, or by telephone, or by a 'letter of agreement', but do not be surprised if your request to fly into the airspace at an unspecified time, place and altitude falls on deaf ears. Clubs that fly near to Class D airspace may have negotiated with the local ATC and have a letter of agreement giving details of the circumstances under which you may enter their airspace, so check with your club and make sure you know the rules *before* you fly.

Class E airspace exists in parts of the Scottish TMA and in Belfast TMA and paragliders are permitted to fly in these areas under full VMC.

Class F airspace is marked on the airmaps as the centre line of a notional 10nm wide airway. There are no restrictions to flying in this airspace, but you should expect higher traffic volumes than in Class G airspace.

Class G airspace is the uncontrolled

Fig 64 Cloudscape – which way to go?

airspace not covered by any of the above where paragliders are free to fly where they wish. Most of your flying will probably be done in Class G airspace.

Flight Levels
The base and top of airspace is marked on the airmaps in flight levels (for example, FL45-FL245). Flight levels are altitudes based on an atmospheric pressure of 1013.2 millibars (or hectopascals), and as such move up and down as the pressure varies. If atmospheric pressure drops to about 997 millibars, FL45 will fall to 4,000ft above sea level, while if it rises to 1030 millibars FL45 will be at 5,000ft AMSL. These are not the altitudes to which you are allowed to fly, however, as air law requires that you maintain a separation of 500ft vertically from airways.

It is difficult to make yourself stop climbing in a good thermal while still 1,000ft from cloudbase, but airline pilots seem to drop just below cloud if they can do so and remain inside their airspace as they approach airports. Milling about at cloudbase in such areas is extremely risky. The lowest flight level you will find on the airmaps will be FL35. If the pressure of the day would cause this to fall below 3,000ft AMSL, this is revised upwards by 500ft to take it back above 3,000ft again.

This 3,000ft mark is known as the transition altitude. Below 3,000 feet, altitudes are expressed as heights above mean sea level, above the transition altitude flight levels are used. You do not really need to know this unless you are being directed by air traffic controllers, which seems unlikely.

It is your responsibility as a pilot to be aware of where you may or may not fly. Your airmaps should be up to date (or at least have the updates drawn on them). Changes to airspace are printed in local magazines and should be noted. If they affect the areas where you may fly, update the info on your maps. Buying new maps once a year is a trivial expense compared to the cost of fuel you will use driving to a site; you may even sometimes find that awkward bits of airspace get removed.

Decisions Based on Airspace

All types of airspace will affect your cross-country flying decisions. You will have taken

Fig 65 Thermalling in company

notice of these hazards, and will have planned a route to avoid as many as possible, but you will not be able to avoid them altogether. The major problem will be large blocks of restricted airspace around large airports. These will extend from the ground upwards (or, in the best case, FL35 upwards), and effectively prevent further progress. You will obviously need to choose a site that will not force you to fly directly towards such airspace.

The next most serious problem is low airways. These reduce the distance of your inter-thermal glides if they are lower than the cloudbase. The lowest airways are at FL35, with a large part of the Midlands being under FL45. Careful planning may suggest that by flying slightly crosswind at some stage in the flight you will be able to avoid low airspace areas, and hence increase your chance of remaining airborne later in the day.

A CROSS-COUNTRY TUTORIAL

Here we will bring the basic skills of thermalling and navigation, as well as the theory concerning max glide and min sink, together into a cross-country tutorial.

When You Get to Base

We have discussed the techniques you will use to get on your way to cloudbase, but have not yet suggested what you should be doing once you get there. You will have spent a good deal of time learning how to get this far and it would be a shame to waste the opportunity for a good flight. Do not let impatience spur you into heading off as soon as you get up to base. Take a look around at the clouds nearest to you as you climb (but only if you can spare the time from concentrating on thermalling; the most important thermal at this stage is the one you are climbing in).

Looking at the Sky

Looking at the clouds every few 360s should show you which ones are growing. Your earlier observation of conditions should give you an idea of how long the clouds are likely to last. Younger, growing clouds will also tend to be a brighter white colour than older decaying clouds, which become more ragged and grey.

Use this information to help you decide whether to head off at once or to drift with your current cloud for a while. Unless the hill you have climbed out from has a very gradual slope on the downwind side of it, or you have been winch-launched from a flat field, there will probably be an area of generally descending air behind the hill. For this reason, it may be prudent to stay with your cloud and drift with it until it starts to decay. Another reason to stay with it is that the sink around the cloud will be greater while the cloud is still producing lift.

It may feel as if the cloud is not drifting at first as it can take a little while for the huge mass of air in a thermal to get up to speed. Do not feel you must hurry along at this early stage. As you gain more experience, you will be able to decide when to race and when to take it easy, but to start with it will often be better to leave it to others to race off in search of more lift.

Scanning the Ground

Scan the ground for thermal sources and thermal triggers. The chances of finding a thermal when you have a thermal source and trigger at the same place are much higher than if you have only one of the two.

Thermal Sources
There is a wide variety of potential thermal sources. These vary from the open-cast coalmines sitting in sunshine to sun-kissed fields

Fig 66 The view from cloudbase

of gently waving wheat. The common aspect of likely sources is that there has been sunshine for long enough to warm the surface air. This need not be for very long in some cases.

A good potential thermal source has the following attributes: it is as dry as possible, has a large surface area to maximize the heating, and a dark colour. Sloping south-facing ground will present a greater area to sunshine than an equivalent piece of flat ground.

High rocky ground or steep scree slopes will be well drained and should warm well, especially if they face into the sun. Towns are also quick to dry, have plenty of surface area, and will warm up well in sunshine. Places that are unlikely to produce good thermals are lakes or marshy ground, or areas with lush vegetation, for example, woodlands or growing crop fields.

Good thermal sources will be at their best if they are surrounded by poor thermal areas. If most of an area is boggy, it is likely there will be general subsidence of the air, which will encourage the areas just away from this sinking air to tend to rise. If a large area is

good for thermal activity, it will be difficult to predict the best spot, as a good thermal rising near by will depress other thermal activity with its associated sink.

If there is only one obvious place to seek your thermal, your task is relatively easy, and you will be more inclined to be prepared to wait for the next thermal cycle from this source if you have nothing else within range. It is always tempting, when finding that your 'obvious' thermal is not there to glide on, to gain an extra kilometre or two. In most cases, though, it is best to wait around to see if something happens; if it doesn't, you will only have lost a couple of kilometres' distance, and the potential benefits to be had by getting back to cloudbase should be worth an occasional failure.

I still have fond memories of the time when I waited over an open-cast coal-mine, slowly sinking towards a gaping hole. The noise of the trucks was starting to get uncomfortably close, when the thermal cycled again and I climbed the 4,000ft back up to base in a beautiful thermal to continue my flight over the Brecon Beacons.

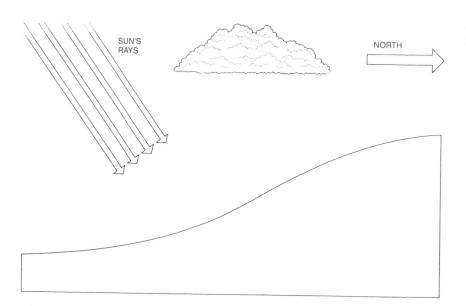

SUN'S RAYS

NORTH

Fig 67 Sunny side thermal

Thermal Triggers

A good thermal trigger is another place to look for a thermal. What you are looking for is something that will disturb the warm layer of air lying over the ground and cause it to break away to form a thermal.

Some of these triggers are permanent features, such as a row of trees, which will cause local turbulence, or the upwind edge of a lake, which will trigger any warm air drifting over the ground into breaking away. Features such as these will be responsible for the majority of 'house' thermals.

Other triggers may be of a more transient nature, and include farm vehicles harvesting wheat or turning over drying cut grass in hay fields, or a cloud shadow moving across the ground. The latter often has quite a good effect, as the cloud may also still be generating its own lift, which will augment the strength of the new thermal source, and may trigger the warm air from a town or open field.

A decaying cloud will also help to trigger the thermal. The descending air will form a small gust front, which will disturb the lower layers of air, causing pockets of warm air to break away from the ground a little way away from the decaying cloud.

It seems that the fixed-location triggers such as trees or lakes produce steady column-type thermals, while the moving cloud shadows tend to release individual pockets of warm air from the ground, giving rise to the doughnut-type thermal.

Advice from Others

Talk to other pilots who regularly fly from the site you intend to use. Hang glider pilots can often provide a good deal of information about where thermals are likely to be found; many have been flying for longer than paraglider pilots have. Also, they have a greater search capacity and will have had the opportunity to look in all sorts of places. Once again, the more information you have at your disposal before you fly, the better the decisions you make in the air are likely to be.

Cloud Streets

A good way of travelling fast is offered by cloud streets. It may be possible to fly straight downwind for several miles with a ground speed of 40 mph or more, without needing to worry about stopping to top up height at every opportunity. Cloud streets will work best if they are not running too closely due north-south. In this direction, the shadow from the clouds will lie directly on the area of ground beneath the streets in the middle of the day, and cut off the source of energy that is keeping them going. The extended areas of lift will be complemented by extended areas of sink between adjacent streets, effectively making it all but impossible for slow gliders to cross from one line of cloud to another until the end of the street is reached.

At this point, you have two choices. You can either glide off towards a nearby street or cloud if there is one close enough to reach, or turn upwind and wait under the end of your current street to see what happens. If you are still finding good lift under the cloud at the end of the street, you can assume that the surrounding sink will still be too strong. Waiting until the street develops further, or

the lift turns to weak sink, would be the best approach in this situation. Another option may be to climb as high as possible inside the clouds and use the extra height to give you the range required to reach the next clouds.

By gliding towards the street to the north of your present position, you will ensure that you pass over the shadowed region of ground while you are still high, and are approaching the next street from the sunny side.

Other Gliders

Probably the best indicator of where a thermal can be found is another glider (of any type) climbing. Think twice before racing off towards them if you are currently in lift. Unless you are high enough to be certain that you will arrive at their thermal at about the same height as they will have climbed to in the time it takes for you to reach them, you should not consider leaving the lift you currently have.

If you arrive even a couple of hundred feet below another glider which is in a doughnut-type thermal, you may well find that you get left behind and hit the deck at the

Fig 68 Cloud streets

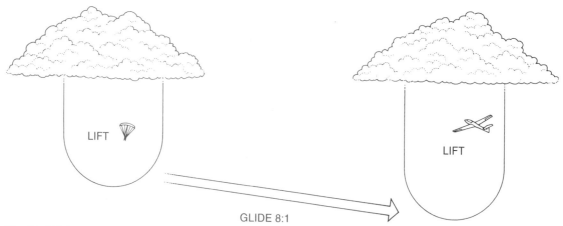

LIFT

LIFT

GLIDE 8:1

Fig 69 Glide towards apparent lift

same time as the other pilot hits cloudbase.

On the other hand, if you are between thermals, there is no question of where you are most likely to connect with your next lift. If the thermal is of the column type, you will not have a problem even if you arrive quite low. Be sure, once you have found some lift, to concentrate on what the air is doing where you are, and not to watch the pilot above you too much.

If there are people catching up with you from below, move over them to try to find the better lift, but, unless you are close below someone who is out-climbing you and was higher to start with, do not try to follow. It is best to forget they are there and focus your attention on coring the best lift where you are. You may find that pilots below you catch you up even though you move over them in search of their better lift. It may be that you have reached the top of the thermal and that your climb rate has therefore slowed down. You will know if it is lack of skill on your part if they carry on climbing past you up to base.

There are actually some advantages to having someone ahead of you in this manner; *see* 'Group Flying' on page 85.

If you do join other thermalling gliders, show them the consideration you would wish

them to show you. Do not ever fly into a thermal at the same height as the pilots already in it without first synchronizing your 360s with theirs. If you are going to arrive just ahead of the other pilot, fly a wider path around the outside until you can join the thermal behind them, ideally on the opposite side of their 360 so that you can both see each other.

If you are joining slightly above a hang-glider or below a sailplane, remember that he may not be able to see you properly. Even with the different flying speeds of paragliders, hang-gliders and sailplanes, it is possible by tightening or opening up your 360s slightly to ensure that you remain opposite the other aircraft right through the 360, and can therefore both keep an eye on each other.

You will obviously join the established circling direction if you are near other gliders. However, what happens if you are in a different core from the others going in the opposite direction, and the two cores migrate towards each other and merge into one? If one core is stronger than the other, the pilots will probably migrate as the cores draw close, and will therefore join the direction of turn in the stronger core. If there are no obvious differences in strength it will prob-

Fig 70 (a) Joining other gliders

Fig 70 (b) Joining other gliders

ably come down to numbers. Use arm signals to let others know that you are about to change direction, and merge with the flow.

Rotation of Thermals

Another common occurrence is when another pilot joins your thermal lower than you, begins circling in his or her favourite direction (which may be the opposite of your direction), and starts to catch you up. The lower aircraft has right of way, so you should change your thermalling direction as they approach, for two good reasons: first, the other pilot will have a more restricted view of you than you have of him; second, there may be a reason why you are being out-climbed. The other pilot may just be a bit of an ace, but

there is a possible alternative; some thermals start to rotate as they climb, like an inverted version of water running down a plughole.

There is no real Coriolis effect acting on the air at this scale of movement, so the direction of rotation is not fixed as it is around weather systems. If you are flying in the opposite direction to the rotation of the thermal, you will take slightly longer to fly a full 360. This means that you will be flying a less banked turn for a 360 of the same size in other words, you will be flying a flatter, more efficient turn in one direction than in the other. Sometimes, the direction of rotation of a thermal can be seen by wind patterns on standing crops or water, or if there is smoke or dust in the air. This is one more thing for you to be looking out for.

Fig 70 (c) Joining other gliders

Gliding

Thermalling takes concentration. Decision-making takes concentration. Collision avoidance takes concentration. Only on glides do you get any real chance to relax a little and your performance will be vastly improved by even a couple of minutes' break. Take a mouthful of your drink, and a snack. Think about something other than flying. You know where you are going and what you will do when you hit lift, and small breaks throughout the flight will enable you to keep alert when you need to be – on the climbs and making your next move decision.

Cloud Flying

It is a privilege to glide in the UK, as it is legal to cloud fly (outside controlled airspace). Cloud flying does not suit everyone; the inside of a cloud is cold and wet, and the lack of all visual reference points can lead to disorientation. If you are susceptible to motion sickness, you may suffer a little. One of the great advantages of a paraglider, however, is that it has much greater pendulum stability than other gliders. This makes it very unlikely that you will find yourself inadvertently looping, as some hang-glider pilots have. You will still lose all sense of direction, however, so a good compass is essential before exploring this new part of the sky.

Given the unwelcoming nature of a cloud, there must surely be a good reason why you should fly in them? There is: climbs will often be two or three times faster inside a cloud than in the thermal up to cloudbase. The key to high average speed is a high climb rate, and so the attraction for a pilot keen to achieve distance is obvious. A further benefit is the increased glide range to be had from the extra few thousand feet available.

It may be best to start to glide out of the lift a little before the freezing level is reached. A damp canopy starting to freeze sounds like a fast way to porosity.

Some sailplane pilots will fly into developing cumulo nimbus clouds in search of fast climbs; many have been hit by lightning, with only minor damage. This is not an option when flying a paraglider; the paraglider pilot cannot pull on 100 knots to get him out of trouble fast. Do not be tempted to fly in clouds unless you are absolutely certain that there is no chance of over-development.

There are a couple of things to look out for here. If a cloud is taller than it is wide, avoid it. Also, if pileus clouds are forming on the developing turrets, assume that this cloud is

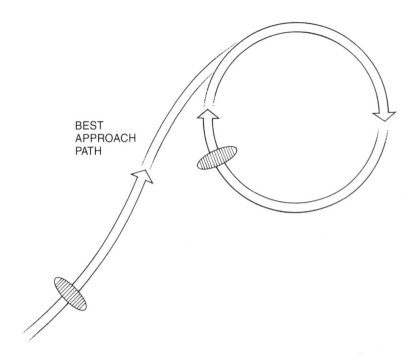

Fig 71 Joining another thermalling glider

BEST
APPROACH
PATH

growing too fast. On a good day for venturing into cloud, look for well-broken cloud cover (so that you can fly out of the side of the cloud when you are high enough), and also look for a capping inversion, making the top of the clouds almost as flat as the bottoms. If the clouds are 2,000 to 4,000ft deep with flat tops you should be safe enough.

So far, comparatively little cloud flying has been done on paragliders, so the best advice is to proceed with caution.

Sea Breezes

If you fly near the coast you will already be familiar with the effect of the sea breeze. It is also important to recognize what the sea breeze looks like from the air to avoid accidentally flying into it. On a good day the sea-breeze front can extend well away from the coast.

The sea air is moist and hazy, and is a

Fig 72 Gliding between thermals

Fig 73 Heading through the clouds

thermal-killer. If you notice that the clouds ahead change from fluffy cumulus into flat sheets, and also that you cannot see towns as far ahead as you could earlier in the flight, you are probably approaching the sea-breeze front. This front will probably have a band of good lift, marked by a line of convergence cloud.

The classic sign of convergence is wispy curtain cloud forming rather lower than cloudbase on the inland side of the frontal zone. If this is not present it is all too easy to fly into the better lift in the convergence region and start to fly faster to capitalize on the better conditions; you may only realize your mistake too late. Once you are in the sea air there is almost no chance of getting back into the good air again.

Fig 74 Sea breeze convergence

Flavour and Style

Every day is slightly different, but there are a number of different *styles* of day, each of which will require a different flying approach to maximize its potential. This is where all the information you have been gathering on your way to the site and up to cloudbase comes together and is used in your first major decision when to leave your first climb. As a rule, you should always take the first climb right up to cloudbase if you can (unless local airspace precludes this). This will give you as full a picture as possible about the rates of climb and drift at any height at which you are likely to fly during the rest of the day.

Good Climb-Out

If the climb has been good all the way up, cloudbase is good and high, and the thermals were cycling regularly on the hill, you should be able race off as soon as you reach cloud-base, confident that you will be able to find another good climb before you get too low. This is a great way to cover distance quickly.

Try to do all your thermalling in the height range where the lift is strongest – if you can do this and still reach the next thermal high enough. For example: you have found that the thermals are strongest above 2,500ft and you are losing 2,000ft on your inter-thermal glides. If you add a small safety margin, you should be confident that if you leave your thermal at 5,000ft you will hit the next one still in the strong lift zone.

(A small note here: you will notice that the inter-thermal glide is measured in height loss. This will apply in all directions if the lift is randomly distributed –in other words, there are no cloud streets. The distance covered over the ground is not a factor. For this reason, your inter-thermal glide speed is irrespective of direction. Many people believe that you must glide faster if heading upwind. This is only true if you are gliding on

to the ground. If you are looking for another thermal, your speed to fly is governed only by your sink rate and polar curve; flying faster will result in you arriving at the next thermal lower and spending more time climbing, drifting as you climb, and hence making slower progress overall.)

If you fail to find the thermal at the expected interval, you will be able to glide the same distance again (note that this refers to distance through the air), and still have 1,000ft above ground level. If you do keep finding thermals nice and high, all will be well, but if you do drop below the strong lift zone, you must stop racing and work anything which is at all useable until you are back in the comfort zone.

Slow Climb-Out

Another style of day will be when the climb out is slow and the thermals are well spaced on the hill. In this case you have little option but to stretch your patience to the limit and drift along in whatever you can find that is not going down. If there is a reasonable drift at base, you will slowly rack up the miles, but only if you fly really conservatively and stay as high as possible all the time.

If you do not seem to be drifting and reach the top of your climb still above the hill, you must look in all directions for your next source of lift. As you are obliged to take your time, take the opportunity to have a good look around at the ground and your airmap, to become completely familiar with the area. This will come in useful on later flights. Even if you know the area well at ground level, things look a little different from base. Keep an eye out for what the sky is doing and be prepared to glide for a forming cloud if the opportunity arises; you can continue your homework later.

Changes During the Day

Most days will not be as clear-cut as this and may start off slowly, pick up into a good racing day later on, and then return to the slow style as the sun gets low in the sky. Be aware of how the day is changing or you will waste the opportunity to cover some serious distance as the day improves, or, worse, find yourself on the ground when there is still another hour of cautious flying left in the sky. If you get good enough at tip-toeing through the weak lift early and late in the day, you will be able to leave earlier and may well have covered twenty or thirty kilometres before the day really starts to go well. If you can extend the flight by the same amount at the end of the day you will really have maximized the day's potential.

Find Out What is Working

To get the best out of a day you want to spend as little time as possible searching for thermals. You can increase your chances of doing this by working out what is working best in the conditions. It may be that you will stay high and be able to fly from cloud to cloud without concerning yourself with ground sources. On other days, you will need to base all your decisions on the ground features.

A growing cloud will have a good firm outline and be brighter white than a decaying one. It is relatively easy to spot good clouds from the ground, but a different matter up at cloudbase. There, your view of the clouds is restricted by the cloud above you, and you will not be able to check the bottom of the other clouds for good dark colour and smooth appearance. A good way of getting another view of your cloud is by looking at its shadow. If there are any holes, you will know there is some sink around. A growing cloud will show up, as the downwind edge of the cloud shadow will be moving across the ground faster than the upwind edge. You may be able to see where a cloud is about to form; a certain milky haze may appear as the top of the thermal approaches

the condensation level. You should also take note of the spot under the cloud where you have the most success, as this will enable you to centre the best lift faster if there is a consistent pattern to the day.

Light Wind Days

There will be days when there is insufficient wind to soar while waiting for thermals to come through. Indeed, there will be days when there is no wind at all between thermal cycles. Days like this can be frustrating, but a little cunning and practice will enable you to make the most of them.

All you need to do is launch just as the thermal starts to break away in front of take-off. It is simple, but if you leave it too late you will catch the post-thermal down-draught of cold air. Some pilots seem to have the knack of always launching just as the lift arrives. This is partly luck, but it is possible to swing the odds in your favour.

The best way to improve your air-time on light wind days is to take off. It may sound obvious, but you will see many pilots sitting around in groups chatting instead of attempting to fly in all wind conditions. Unless it is not possible to slope-land at your chosen site, the worst that will happen is that you will have a short walk if you fail to launch into lift.

If you remain in your harness, with the glider spread out ready to launch, you will be able to take immediate advantage of any thermals. As soon as the canopy starts to rustle slightly in the thermal breeze, you should be launching. If you are standing up and ready to launch, you will be ahead of the game.

There are two ways of being ready for this launch window: stand ready to launch all the time, or keep your ears open for one beep from your vario. A fellow pilot pointed out to me that his vario would beep once just before the thermal breeze started. One possible reason for

Fig 75 (a) Busy thermal

this is that, as the thermal breaks away upwards in front of the hill, there is a slight pressure drop, and this is just enough to make the vario beep once. This is your cue to get ready to launch, as the breeze will be on the hill in a few seconds. If the site you are at is high enough, an alpine launch at this point would get the absolute maximum from the thermal.

If there is just enough wind to pop your canopy up, but not enough to allow you to soar, you will be able to detect the arrival of a thermal either by the canopy lifting more, or by the canopy trying to over-fly you. This second effect is caused by the canopy trying to maintain its normal angle of attack, while the airflow is directed more vertically by the thermal.

You may find yourself having to apply a considerable amount of brake to stop the canopy surging too far forward, but you will probably not feel a great increase in lift. Learn to recognize the signs and have the confidence to launch when you feel them.

Once you have launched and start to climb, you will need to spend as much time as possible in the core of the thermal, so you should start to 360 as soon as it is safe to do so. Tight S' bends are a safer option until you

are certain you have the space to start your 360s. There are few better feelings than climbing up above a group of fellow pilots who are still sitting on the hills trying to work out your secret.

GROUP FLYING

A cross-country flight can be made more interesting and easier by flying as a group of two or more, and working together to improve the chances of locating a thermal and coring the lift quickly. A larger group of co-operating pilots will be able to fly faster and stay higher, and hence will fly further.

Techniques

One of the obvious ways to improve the chances of locating the next thermal on a glide is to have several pilots spread out to cover a much larger sweep of sky. If more than one of the pilots finds lift at about the same time, each should concentrate on his or her own area until it becomes apparent which pilot is climbing best.

This simple approach can be refined further to increase the chance of each member of the group being able to reach the lift once it has been found. If the glide is at all crosswind, the highest pilot should fly the furthest downwind and the lowest furthest upwind. In this way, if the pilot furthest upwind finds the lift, the pilot who has furthest to glide also has the greatest height and hence a good chance of reaching the thermal before hitting the ground. If the lowest pilot has to make a long into-wind glide, there is a greater chance he or she will not make it, and the group will be reduced in number.

Another technique can enable a group to climb better once a thermal has been found, especially when the core is weak and ill defined. One (or more if there are plenty of you) pilot should stay in what weak lift there is, while others fly occasional extended loops

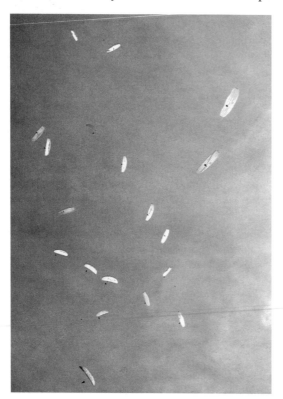

Fig 75 (b) Busy thermal

in a search pattern to determine if there is a better core somewhere close by. The pilot remaining with the established lift will serve as a marker of where the exploring pilot(s) should return if they do not find the better lift. In many cases, where the lift is weak and widespread there may be several cores of varying strengths. In these conditions the searching should continue for the whole climb, unless a particularly strong core is found to maximize the climb rate.

The faster you climb, the sooner you can glide and hence the further you will be able to fly. Use the strengths of the group to keep the pace up when conditions are good and to keep high when things are not so strong. You will need to be aware of 'gaggle drag', where all the pilots end up circling in an area after the lift has gone, for the simple reason that others are still circling and (so the reasoning goes) there *must* be some lift about somewhere.

When the lift gets very weak and broken you should check your altimeter occasionally; intermittent bleeps from the vario may suggest that you are slowly gaining height, while in reality you may be gently sinking out. If there are any likely thermal sources within gliding range, now would be a good time to head for them. If all is gloom, however, it may be best to stay put if you are only sinking slowly until a patch of sunshine appears or some other sign of lift is spotted.

Radios

A further enhancement to the benefits of flying as a group and to the enjoyment of the flight can be made by good use of radios. They can be used for discussing what to do next and for attracting attention when you find lift. State who you are and what the lift is like (preferably giving an average reading if your vario has an averager function), for example, 'This is Matthew, and I'm in an average three up.' Even if there are just two of you, calling your name helps to ensure you are not listening to other pilots whom you cannot see but who are in radio range.

Radios can also be used as a safety aid if you decide to enter cloud with other pilots. If each pilot calls their altitude at intervals it will be possible to avoid collisions by ensuring that you maintain a good vertical separation from the other pilot(s). (Generally, it is better to avoid cloud flying except when you are on your own or with maybe one other pilot; in any case, keep in contact all the time you are in the cloud.)

Radios are also useful for retrieve organization, especially when flying overseas. Extended aerial lengths will improve communications on the ground, as will placing the car aerial in the middle of the car roof. As the reception will be better from the air, it is a good idea to keep the retrieve crew aware of where you are likely to be before you get too low. You can always call back to cancel the message if you get another climb. It is also good practice to use a different channel for the retrieve calls from the flying channel to avoid unnecessary traffic distracting pilots during their flying.

PRE-PLANNING

Planning a cross-country flight is a multi-stage process, encompassing everything from winter dreaming to choosing a good landing field at the end of the day. Prior planning will help you to make much better decisions 'on the fly'; even the choice of where to seek your next thermal comes under the planning umbrella.

Forecast and Site

You will know which of your local sites is best for a given wind direction. Consider joining other clubs further afield (many offer associate membership for members of other clubs), to maximize the potential for a given wind direction. There are two major factors that limit distance potential in the UK: low airspace and the coast both of which may mean you have to travel in search of the maximum. If your local sites are restrictive in certain wind directions, spend some time studying the airmaps for sites within reasonable travelling distance which offer greater scope. It is probably only worth a long drive if the wind is from one of the better directions basically west through to north-east.

Track, Hazards and Goals

Once you have selected a suitable starting point for a given wind direction, you should be able to form an idea of the cone of probability for your track: in other words, a wedge shape extending downwind from the site, representing the limits of your potential track.

Once the cone of probability is established, check the area for any major airspace problems mainly airspace that drops below FL45. ATZs and MATZs are not necessarily major problems as on a good day they may be flown over (leaving a good safety margin at all times). If a MATZ is quiet, you are technically allowed to fly through it unless prevented by local by-laws (but not its enclosed ATZ). Problem areas that are not related to airspace should also be planned around. One obvious example is a large river, where the sea breeze may advance a long way inland up the river valley, and the river itself will tend to encourage lush vegetation that is not good for thermals.

When you have narrowed down your intended track to avoid low airspace, check the map again, looking for easily recognizable features which can help you to pinpoint your position. If there is some airspace you

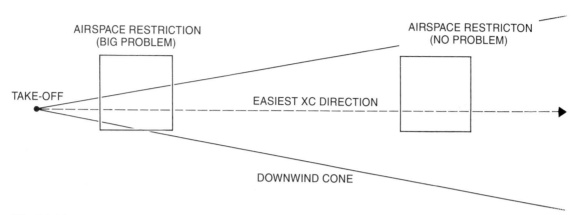

Fig 76 Airspace restrictions, near and far

must fly near, but need to stay out of, be certain to check for ground features which define the edge of the airspace in question – a major road, bridge or distinctive road junction, or perhaps a village or lake. It is much easier to prepare at home than at base after two or three hours' flying. It is also much more relaxing to approach a hazard knowing how you are going to pass it rather than having to worry about it as it gets closer; this way, you will be able to concentrate on staying high.

It may also be worth considering possible routes back home while you are at this planning stage. You will probably want the option of a quick retrieve. It is difficult to end up very far from a town in the UK (with the exception, perhaps, of parts of Scotland), but if you feel that you are within easy distance of a major road, you will be far less likely to opt to land early rather than pushing on. Every extra boost to your confidence will help you on the big day, so it is worth considering as much as you can before you head for the hill.

Equipment

It is best to prepare as much of your gear as you can the night before you fly. Check the strength of your vario battery, radio batteries, and mobile phone batteries, and replace or recharge them if they are getting low. Fill your ballast bag if you use one. (Some pilots pack two ballast bags in the car; if they bomb out on the first attempt they can dump the ballast for the journey back to the hill and still have a full ballast bag for the next attempt.) Make sure that you have money for telephone calls and bus or train (or air!) fares that may be necessary. Make sure that your drinking water container is clean and filled. (If necessary, this can be cleaned with Milton baby bottle sterilizing tablets.) If you like to eat on long flights, sort out your rations now as well.

Your glider, harness and reserve should all be in the bag. Do not forget your helmet, boots and gloves, and plenty of warm clothing to wear under your flying suit. On cold days some pilots fly with hand warmers. These resemble tea bags and contain activated charcoal that gets warm when removed from the airtight packaging and will stay warm for about eight hours. They only work once, so ensure you have a fresh set packed (and that the packaging is still airtight). Have the correct airmap in your map case, as well as some pages from a road atlas to help you find your way back – make sure it shows all the minor roads – and a list of the phone numbers of people who may be able to help with a retrieve.

One of the most important pieces of equipment that you need to prepare for your planned flight is yourself. Huge distances have been made by pilots with hangovers, but even greater distances may have been possible if the pilots had been in better repair! Eat sensibly, drink water or fruit juice rather than beer or spirits, and retire to bed early – tomorrow is a big day.

Preparing for Take-Off

Try to develop a routine for your preparations to include all your pre-flight checks. Do not allow yourself to be interrupted. If you want to chat with friends before flying, do it either before or after checking your kit; one day, you may miss something. Try to find a space away from others in which to prepare and use the time to get in the right mental state too, especially in competitions or other high-pressure situations; these might include a day when your family or non-flying friends have come to watch.

Fold your map for the day. If you anticipate a good day, try folding your map to show twice the area your map case will hold before folding it in half and putting it in the map case. This will make it much easier to get to the needed bit of map if you have to swap it around in the air. A couple of paper clips will also help to stop it flapping into a mess in the air.

PLANNING LANDINGS

A simple and obvious rule of thumb about landing is never to fly somewhere where you cannot glide to a landing area. At cloudbase you will be able to glide to fields which may be 10km or more downwind from your posi-

tion; this will provide plenty of safe landing opportunities in the UK. Avoid landing in fields where there are farm animals, which may be disturbed by your unexpected arrival, or where there are crops standing. (This includes grass, which in many parts of the country is grown as winter fodder for farm animals.) Paragliders frequently rely upon the goodwill of the farming community, so always try to pick a field where you will cause the minimum of inconvenience. There is also the chance that if you land near to some buildings, you may be invited in and allowed to use the telephone.

General Advice

Always make sure your options are open. If you are flying in an area where landings are restricted (for example, over a town), be sure you have a site you can always reach. Check that the field you have spotted is free from power lines. Ensure that there are no large obstacles too close upwind which may cause rotor just where you do not need it. Another potential hazard in this situation is that if the field is on the small side, and you fly into the wind shadow behind trees or large buildings; you may find yourself out-gliding the field with your suddenly increased forward speed. Check again for power lines. Have an approach planned that will avoid passing over fields containing livestock, especially in the spring.

Specific Advice

While you have plenty of height (say 1,000ft or so), you can afford to be fairly relaxed about which field you select for landing, but as you drop lower you should choose the best-looking field and head for it. If you have a choice of good fields, the best one will be that which you will fly over the greatest number of potential thermal sources to get to – just because you are making sure you have a safe place to land does not mean you should stop trying to get back up again. You should also be looking around for signs of which way the wind is blowing. Flags and smoke are excellent indicators. Wind patterns on water are also useful (the upwind side will normally be flatter calm than the rest, and any gusts should be seen tracking across the surface). If there are no obvious indicators, flying a few 360s and noting the drift will give you an idea. Knowing which way the wind is coming from is important not only for the actual touchdown, but for assessing the suitability of a field with regard to turbulence problems.

Definite Advice

Once you have chosen your landing field, stick with the decision unless you have plenty of time to check the alternatives (in which case you may have decided too high up). Do not try to hop just one field more once you are below about 200 feet. One pilot did this, turned into wind to land, saw the power lines at the last moment as they rose above the skyline, and broke his arm in an avoidance manoeuvre.

Options

If you find you arrive at your selected field with plenty of height in hand to reach a field further on, feel free to do so if you have checked it out. As it becomes clear that you are going to arrive at the first choice nice and high, start looking for a good alternative further on while you are in the less demanding straight glide part of the

approach and do not need to crane your neck to look at a field over your shoulder. The sooner and higher you make this decision the safer you should be as you have more time to spot power lines. Like most of the hazards you will find on landing, power lines are only a problem if you have not seen them. Plan ahead, look carefully, and you should land safely.

POST-FLIGHT ANALYSIS

Once you have landed and made your way back home there is still more you can do to improve your cross-country skills. Unless you have just completed a defined task or have run out of land to fly over, you could almost certainly have flown a little (or, indeed, a great deal) further. You should spend some time looking back on the flight and working out where your mistakes happened. This may sound negative, but the intention is to improve your decision-making on subsequent flights.

If there were still clouds popping after you landed, you should look at your thermal source selection skills, or perhaps you were trying to fly too fast. If you manage to keep flying until all thermal activity has ended, you cannot afford simply to pat yourself on the back. There may well have been a period during the flight when you should have been flying faster. Even with completed defined flights, you may ask yourself if you should have set a more ambitious task. If you reach the coast, could you have increased the possible distance by flying some crosswind legs earlier in the day? Take your time and learn from your mistakes. You will always learn better lessons from your own mistakes than by listening to others.

5 Theory of Gliding

VARIO MEASUREMENTS

Airspeed

Advanced gliding theory relies on the ability to measure airspeed accurately when flying. This is very difficult with a paraglider, for two reasons. First, the glider actually travels very slowly, and the mechanics of measuring the airspeed therefore need to be quite precise. Second, the airspeed sensor is normally close to the pilot, whereas, theoretically, it is the airspeed of the wing that needs to be measured. With a gap of approximately seven metres between pilot and wing, and the pilot swinging, especially when turning, it is not often that both will be doing exactly the same speed. However, having the sensor a good distance from the wing will prevent the airspeed measured being affected by the aerodynamics around the aerofoil.

Total Energy

When in gliding flight, the only direct control the pilot has over his sink rate in the air is by changing the airspeed of the glider. As the pilot slows, so the glider will climb, and vice versa. The theory is that the glider has potential energy, in the form of altitude, and kinetic energy, in the form of airspeed. As the glider dives, it will exchange some of its potential energy (height) for an increase in kinetic energy (speed). This kinetic energy is then available to be converted back into potential energy, purely by slowing the wing. Therefore, the original height loss in a dive does not represent sinking air, and any sink reading from the vario can be regarded as misleading. The same is true, of course, if the glider is slowed, and subsequently climbs.

This relationship between airspeed and available energy can be compensated for by setting the vario up to measure airspeed as well as sink rate. A calculation circuit is included in the electronics that will adjust the vario reading should the speed change. This is known as Total Energy Compensation.

Airmass Vario

The polar curve for a glider will give values for the sink rate at various airspeeds. If the vario is able to store the values from the polar curve as well as measure the airspeed, it can work out at what rate the glider would be expected to be sinking if the air was stationary. Any differences between this and the actual sink rate would be related to vertical movement of the air, and not to the airspeed of the glider. If the vario displays this value, it is known as an airmass vario.

The airmass vario is particularly useful when gliding at speed, where the sink rate of the glider is quite high, and could mask any weak, but useful lift through which the glider passes.

It should be noted that an airmass vario will read zero lift/sink when the glider is flying in still air, whereas a vario set up in the normal way would give the glider's sink rate. The airmass vario is therefore of little use when thermalling, only when gliding. To allow for this, some manufacturers include an automatic switch in the instrument so that as soon as the vario registers a climb it is 'normal', and in sink it changes to 'airmass'.

Speed to Fly

The value of max glide speed changes depending on whether the glider is flying into or downwind, or whether the air is lifting or sinking.

If the vario has the ability to store and recall values from the polar curve, it is possible for it to compute the best speed for the pilot to fly, with regard to the vario lift/sink reading, if a speed probe is fitted. Should the glider be in sinking air, the best speed would be faster than max glide, and the vario would indicate that the pilot should speed up. This is called a 'speed to fly calculator' and gives the best glide through the air. It will be used when gliding to a cloud, when the important factor is to arrive at a different position in the airmass, rather than to cover the maximum distance over the ground. This simple approach is developed further by using the McCready ring.

Changing the best speed to fly with regard to whether the pilot is trying to fly into wind or downwind, has, up until recently, had to rely on a manual input from the pilot of an approximate wind strength. With the advent of small, cheap GPS receivers, this calculation can now be done by the vario, assuming a suitable GPS interface. (*See* page 93 for more about GPS.)

McCready Speed to Fly

Flying the glider at max glide is a good 'safe' option, as you will arrive at the next thermal with the maximum height possible. If there is a sufficient margin available, it is possible to improve your overall speed by flying faster than the max glide speed. Flying faster means that you will reach the thermal lower, but

Fig 77 Gliding at speed

sooner. If you gain more height by climbing in this saved time than the amount you lost by flying faster, you will be at an advantage.

The amount of height you can afford to lose, and thus the amount by which you can increase your speed, is proportional to the expected strength of the next thermal. (It is important to use the average climb rate for this. A vario may well be showing '8 up' for much of the time on the main display, but only '5 up' on the averager.) This technique was developed by Paul McCready and originally consisted of a perspex dial, which the pilot rotated to the value of the anticipated next climb.

Modern electronic varios display a secondary pointer, which indicates the climb rate given your speed. This 'backwards' approach means you vary your speed to make the pointer move to the value you expect for the climb. The result is the same, with a different starting point. As an example, imagine a situation where two identical gliders are at base together. They both set off on a glide to a likely looking cloud, one gliding at max glide, the other 5 mph faster. By the time the slower glider gets to the next thermal, the faster one (who got there lower but more quickly) has climbed higher and is now nearer base. If the two gliders carried on in the same way, the quicker glider would fairly soon pull out a considerable lead.

GPS

So far we have only considered how to obtain the maximum glide performance in an airmass. The theories are equally true for all wind directions. It is not true that you should fly faster into wind when gliding to a climb; you will arrive lower and spend more time climbing and drifting back downwind. In order to get the maximum distance over the ground, you need to know what effect the wind is having. This is where GPS comes in.

If the thermal source you are heading for is not a cloud drifting at the same speed as the airmass, but a fixed source such as a peak or a town, you will need to fly faster into wind, or may fly slower downwind than would otherwise be the case. The ground speed from the GPS, combined with the airspeed from the vario, gives a more useful speed to fly for these situations. For mountain flying this will be the majority of the time. Even for the

drifting thermals, this approach has some benefits, as the thermal may well be drifting at a slower speed than the rest of the airmass, having started as stationary air on the ground. It takes a while for such a large body of air to get up to speed.

The McCready calculation will still be applied to vary the optimum speed to compensate for the expected climb rate, and the same display is likely to be used. For the maximum distance over the ground you will then fly with an expected climb of zero.

Some speed to fly calculators allow the pilot to enter an estimate for the drift speed of the thermal they are heading for, while others may assume that the thermal is stationary. Know which way your vario performs the calculation and adjust the speed to fly it suggests accordingly.

RULE OF THUMB

If you are starting to despair because your vario is not linked to NASA's computers, don't. The performance gains to be made by using the above systems to the full provide a useful improvement over simply flying at a steady speed; however, simply flying faster in the sink and when gliding towards upwind 'slow' thermals, you will gain almost all the possible performance. It can feel as if you are overdoing the speed as your sink rate increases rather markedly, but the best speed to fly through sink is faster than you would imagine. Fortunately, large areas of sinking air through which you find yourself gliding are normally turbulence-free, so the speed bar can be used without too much worry of a major collapse.

6 Instruments

You will use various instruments when flying, especially cross country. They help you with thermalling, navigation and, more recently, optimizing glider performance.

ALTIMETERS

An altimeter is an instrument that tells you your height or altitude. It is essential, especially in situations where you have to navigate either above or below controlled airspace.

All altimeters work by measuring pressure, with the assumption that pressure changes at a set rate with respect to altitude. Fortunately, this is the case in the lower atmosphere where paragliders fly. Measuring pressure is reasonably simple, and can be done either mechanically or electronically.

Mechanical Altimeters

All easily transportable mechanical altimeters work on the aneroid principle. The theory is that a sealed container will expand or contract, depending on whether the outside pressure decreases or increases. This expansion can be converted into a movement of a pointer by a simple series of levers. Thus as the altimeter is raised so the external pressure reduces, and the pointer shows the degree of pressure difference. This can easily be calibrated to read directly in feet or metres.

The instruments mostly used by paraglider pilots are the hand-held pocket-sized altimeters primarily built for climbers and walkers. As they are mechanical, the quality of construction is critical for accuracy. The more expensive types have 3,000ft for each full rotation of the dial; this is reasonably precise, but difficult to read quickly. Cheaper ones have as much as 10,000ft per rotation, which is easy to read, but only to the nearest 200ft or so.

Mechanical altis have gone a little out of fashion recently because most electronic varios have a built-in altimeter, which is electronic and often precise to the nearest three or ten feet. As it does not need batteries, and is reasonably robust, the mechanical instrument can, however, be very useful as a back-up.

Electronic Altimeters

Electronic altimeters rely on electronic sensors to measure the pressure changes, and normally use an LCD display calibrated to give the altitude. As with a mechanical alti, the accuracy relates directly to the quality of the components. They normally resolve to either 3ft (1m) or 10ft (3.5m), and are almost universally more precise than accurate.

Most electronic altis are only available as part of a combined vario/altimeter, as the same pressure sensor is used for both applications. Some wrist watches also now have an altitude sensor built in, but these are of little use to us as they are very imprecise, and slow to update to changes in altitude.

Choosing an Altimeter

Most altis are part of a vario, so you are less likely to be concerned about the quality of the alti than the vario itself. If you are looking for a stand-alone alti, look for one that is easy to read quickly, and that updates reasonably rapidly. There is a limited choice in both electronic and mechanical models.

Accuracy

Because all altis measure pressure, and atmospheric pressure is seldom constant for any length of time, the altimeter has to be set at a known altitude at the beginning of each flying day. No matter how good the instrument, if the original setting is wrong the alti will always be inaccurate.

VARIOMETERS

Variometers measure rate of change of altitude, and will thus give a direct indication of whether the glider is climbing or sinking, and how fast it is doing it. As with altimeters, there are both mechanical and electronic varios, although the mechanical ones are rare enough now that they are practically museum pieces.

Mechanical Varios

The mechanical vario relied upon air flowing into or out of a container or flask, as it was lowered or raised. As the vario was raised, the air would flow out of the flask to equalize the pressure. Various methods were used to give a visual representation of the air movement. In the most basic vario, the airflow pushed lightweight pith balls up tubes, one tube for climb, and one for sink. Despite their somewhat crude workings, these 'flask' varios are extremely accurate and quick, and are still commonly used in sailplanes.

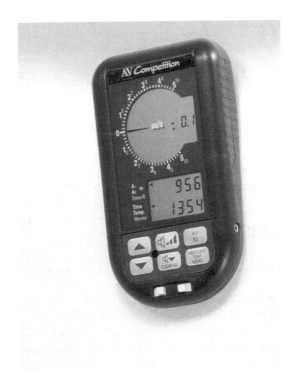

Fig 78 Modern variometer and altimeter

Electronic Varios

The electronic vario uses the same pressure sensors as an electronic altimeter, with the addition of an integrator circuit to give rate of change. This information is displayed visually, either with an LCD or needle, and audibly. Your choice of vario depends on a number of factors.

Features
There is a vast range of varios and vario/altis available, from simple and cheap to very complicated. Common features found as options include (but are no means restricted to):

· Vario, vario/alti or vario/alti/a.s.i.
· 1, 2 or 3 altis, for QNH, QFE and QNE
· LCD display or needle
· Volume, on/off, and thresholds on sound

- Averager
- Previous peak value memory/memories

On the more complicated instruments the options may include:

- Barograph
- Total energy
- Speed to fly/airmass/polar curve calculators
- McCready computers
- GPS interface, actual glide computers

Audio
The actual noise the vario makes is probably the most important thing to consider when purchasing. Think about the climb and the sink tone, the volume and the adaptability. Is it possible to set the sink tone threshold, and/or turn it off completely with ease? Remember that if you use a flight deck, the volume will need to be quite high, whereas if you use a harness mount you might want it quite low.

Ease of Use
Choose a vario that is relatively easy to use. Once it is set up with all the options you want, you should not have to go through a lengthy procedure each time you turn it on.

COMPASS

Although electronic compasses have become available over the past few years, the mechanical ones are still favoured by most pilots. This is primarily because the electronic ones give an erroneous reading when they are not held reasonably level, whereas a good-quality mechanical one will work at any angle.

There are two main types of mechanical compass, flat and spherical. The flat compass has the same problem as the electronic one it will not work unless held reasonably level so the pilot knows he always has to do something to get a reading. Some are better damped than others; it is worth trying to find

Fig 79 Instrument deck, with vario, compass and map

one designed for orienteering rather than just hill walking, as these are quicker to settle.

There is also a range in the quality of the damping in spherical compasses. As a general rule, the bigger the compass ball the better, but it is worth swinging the compass about and seeing how quick it is to settle down before purchase. Generally, good spherical compasses are expensive, but well worth the extra cost. If you are considering cloud flying, a good spherical compass is invaluable.

RADIOS

Radios are either legal to use from the air ('airband'), or not legal for airborne transmission (two-metre band). Unfortunately, there are so many advantages to a two-metre band radio (mostly that it is cheap and actually works), that if you were to turn up at your local flying site with an airband transceiver, you might find nobody there to talk to.

There are airband frequencies dedicated to glider pilots for in-flight use, and even one restricted just to hang gliders and paragliders. These frequencies are the only ones you can use without a full RT licence. 129.9MHz, 129.975MHz, 130.1MHz, 130.125MHz and 130.4MHz are the frequencies that have been allocated to gliders; paragliders are officially all classed as 'gliders'. Unfortunately, all the other gliding traffic also uses them, so quite a lot of congestion should be expected. The new frequency that has been allocated is 118.675MHz, and this should be restricted to just paragliders and hang gliders.

All airband radios are AM, just like medium wave on your old radio, and they share the same problems of poor quality and unreliable transmission. However, they do have a range that is not restricted to 'line of sight'.

The two-metre band radios used by paragliders are designed to work in the amateur band 144-145MHz and because there is quite a big market they are reasonably cheap. We tend not to use them within this band (you need a licence, and are still unable to transmit from the air), but close to it, normally between 143.85MHz and 143.975MHz. There does not seem to be much traffic on these frequencies at the moment, but this may be about to change.

These radios work on the FM, so quality is normally very good, but range is restricted to line of sight, except in exceptional weather conditions. The only time you are likely to need a radio when you cannot actually see the receiver is after landing after a cross-country flight, when you are calling your retrieve vehicle. Most pilots will carry a long telescopic aerial to help in these conditions.

Two-metre band radios are used in most countries in mainland Europe, and extensively in the Alps. It is not legal to transmit from the air anywhere, but the authorities generally seem to turn a blind eye (or ear). Indeed, there have certainly been so many occasions in the Alps where the use of a radio has saved a life, that a clampdown would be likely to cause a considerable outcry.

There is talk of some dedicated two-metre frequencies around the 137MHz area being allocated to hang glider and paraglider pilots. We await developments. All present radios would still work, although some aerial re-tuning might be desirable for best performance.

GPS Global Positioning Systems

Global positioning systems (or SatNav or GNSS) units are now so cheap and accurate that they are becoming a great boon even to the occasional cross-country pilot. There are drawbacks, but a system that tells you instantly where you are, how fast you are going, and the direction in which you are heading, must be invaluable.

There are various choices you need to make before buying a GPS. Depending on what you are prepared to pay, you can get a receiver with airspace information already programmed in, various sizes of moving map displays, and even various colours on the display. Below are some of the features you might consider.

1. Ease of use. A GPS has many functions and features. Is it reasonably intuitive what it will do when you press each button?
2. Cost and development. Much like personal computers, GPS technology is a fast-moving area. Shop around.
3. Airspace information database. You can pay over double the price for a receiver that has a built-in airspace database, and you will pay a fair amount of money each year to keep it updated. On most GPSs the display is little more than an inch and a half wide, and all the information contained on your 1:500,000 colour airmap on a little black and white screen is difficult to interpret. GPSs will not yet run for more than about ten hours on one set of batteries, so it is still absolutely essential to carry an up to date paper airmap. You might prefer to save your money and choose not to have the airspace database.
4. Connection to a variometer. Most vario manufacturers now do a top of the range instrument that will input information directly from your GPS to display your actual glide, as well as wind speed and direction, and required glide/actual glide comparison. If you plan to use one of these instruments, your GPS must have the appropriate output. Currently, most GPS access variometers require NMEA 183 protocol.

The main cost of all the useful information that a GPS will give you is the amount of power it will consume. Unlike a vario, which will do most of a season on one set of AA batteries, a GPS will get through four in about ten hours. If you use the GPS to navigate to the hill, as well as in the air, it is well worth considering rechargeables and an in-car charger. You can also get a solar cell to run the GPS, especially designed for cars and hang gliders, but at a cost (about 150 hours of batteries).

7 Competition Flying

INTRODUCTION

There are many aspects in common between recreational cross-country flying and flying against other pilots in competitions. All the techniques used to fly far or fast will still apply in competition, but the balance of caution against speed will change and almost all tasks flown in competitions these days will be defined races rather than open distance flying. You do not need to be fiercely competitive to enjoy the atmosphere and flying of competition. Flying a task set by someone else can be an eye-opening experience, initially perhaps because it shows you just how far and fast the experts can go, and will inspire you to do it too!

The main difference between recreational flying and competition flying is that you will not be able to choose when to launch and which way to go. This applies equally to all the pilots and should be seen as an extra challenge. The positive side is that there will be a larger number of good pilots all flying at the same site, which will provide you with the best thermal markers. It is no coincidence that many of the best flights are flown in competitions.

STEPS TO SUCCESS

Preparation

There are a number of steps you can take to improve your chances of success. Preparation is the key. You will have only a limited amount of time between arriving at the site and the task window being opened, and a briefing will take up a chunk of this time too.

When you arrive at the site, you will need to get yourself into the best position for a good take-off. Some may be happy to join the bunfight for the prime take-off point (or the front of the queue if there is a queue system in action), while others will benefit more by selecting a quieter spot in which to prepare. You should check your canopy before bunching it up in case you need to move a little, and load your harness with your drinking water and ballast, and so forth. Check your radio if you will be using it in the air. Set your altimeter too. If you have two altimeters, consider setting the second one to show zero in the goal field if you can. (Note that by two altimeters we mean a vario with two altimeter displays – any back-up alti-vario should be set in the normal fashion to ensure you do not stray into airspace by mistake.) This will be very useful information when you are judging your glide into goal.

Equipment

Below is a selection of items that may prove useful in competitions.

Carrying a back-up vario can save the day if the batteries in your main one pack up in mid flight. (You may put in new batteries for the competition, but sometimes you may just have a dud.) A cheap second-hand basic alti-vario is ideal; barograph traces and GPS interfaces are not the main consideration at this time. Do not forget to set the altimeter of the back-up vario at launch when you set the main.

A Post-It pad is useful, both for any telephone numbers or notes that you need to write down, as well as for reminders you might wish to place on your map for reference during the flight. For example, you may want to have a list of the required photo sequence visible during the flight, or mark and number the turnpoints and goal field using small pieces torn off the pad. The sticky backing stops all these notes sliding around the map and getting in the way. Do not forget a pen (also useful for getting landing witnesses names).

The Briefing

Once you have prepared your flying kit, prepare for the briefing. Take your map, map case, camera(s) and a notepad with you to the briefing. You will need to note down telephone numbers (to report in as landed safe), and may wish to make notes to clarify turnpoint details and photo sequences. Mark the turnpoints and the photographic sector required either directly on the map, or on the map case using an overhead projector pen or chinagraph pencil. If you are writing on the map case, ensure that the map cannot slide around in the map case causing your markers to appear in the wrong places. Some pilots use tape or Blutac for this. Make sure you know where the turnpoints are and what they look like, and also which side of them you should be on for the all-important turnpoint photo. If you are unsure of something, ask the meet director (or 'meat-head', as they are always known) before the briefing is closed.

Fig 80 Competition launch

Just Before the Start

There is now a short waiting period before the task window is declared open. To achieve their best performance, most competitors will need to be a little keyed up. However, if you are very nervous, take time out to calm down and relax a little or you will be unable to concentrate sufficiently on your flying. At the other extreme, if you are completely relaxed, try to psych yourself up to get the level of drive required for optimum performance. The same effect applies when you are free flying too, but most people will find they are quite relaxed in this situation.

When to Launch

Your first major decision, when you should launch, now needs to be made. If you do it too soon, you run the risk of sinking out; too late, and you will be left behind and may run out of time before you can reach the goal field. A large number of pilots will be watching to see

Fig 81 Waiting for the start to open

when the aces make their move and will all try to launch at once to follow them. This will just lead to you being caught in a mob low down at the start, and the fast pilots will soon leave you behind. A better approach is to take off as soon as you feel sure you will be able to stay up. This will give you the height and space to enable you to follow the hotshots as they catch up and pass you.

Tactics

It can be very tempting to leave a thermal earlier than you normally might, because you are racing and feel that you should therefore be going as fast as possible. However, you must remember that it is a race to goal. The big points are for reaching goal (or getting very close), and the speed points are then a bonus. It is better to fly a little too cautiously than a little too fast. You should also remember that the inter-thermal distance will be proportional to the convective depth. In other words, if you do not climb to the top of the thermal, but leave half-way up, you may well not reach the next thermal. As an

example, a hang glider pilot in a competition overseas left a climb after 5,000ft. He failed to find another thermal, while the pilots who remained in the original climb topped out at nearly 10,000ft.

Try to stay with a gaggle if you can. You will have a far better chance of finding lift and centring it rapidly. You do not need to win a task by a huge margin to win a competition, but if you strike out on your own all the time you are much more likely to bomb out on at least one task which will put you out of contention. Even if you feel the gaggle is missing an opportunity, you should remain with the group unless you are more than 75 per cent certain that you will reach goal by this other course; if the chance is anything less than this, you should stay with the group. You need a margin as wide as this to compensate for losing the improved thermal-finding capacity of the group.

On a long task you may find yourself flying alone after a long time in the air. You may be getting tired, and it is tempting in this circumstance to feel that you have done well enough and pick a place to land. Try to picture yourself on the ground watching

Fig 82 Busy competition launch

another glider drifting past overhead. This should provide you with the motivation to keep on working in any dregs of lift that you may find.

TURNPOINT PHOTOS

You will almost certainly need to take turnpoint photos during competition tasks. These will normally be required to show that you were in the FAI turnpoint sector (*see* Fig 83).

There are a number of pitfalls that you will need to avoid in order to convince the judges that you were in the correct place. First, you should have a camera that is working properly. For serious pilots this means carrying two cameras and taking all photos with both to minimize the chance of a technical problem robbing you of your points. Many

will choose totally manual cameras with no batteries to fail in the low temperatures encountered at altitude. You should also be certain that the film is loaded correctly.

Once you have a working camera or two and have flown into the required sector you can still make silly mistakes. A finger over the lens is quite common, and a leg or harness obscuring the turnpoint will also result in a probable loss of points. Unless you are clearly right in the middle of the sector, the picture can suggest you are further in or out than you are, depending on the position of the turnpoint in the frame.

GLIDING TO GOAL

You will need to perfect the art of gliding to goal. The perfect glide will see you crossing the line with just enough height to enable you to land into wind. To help with this you should set the second altimeter so that it will read zero in the goal field so you know how much height you have to play with. Marking circles on your map to show the 5km and 10km to go lines, or alternatively the altitude you will need at certain easily identifiable points on your track, will also help with judging glides.

This information can be used in conjunction with various levels of high-tech gadgetry. If you estimate your glide angle you can use a look-up table to check what height you need to reach goal from the 5km mark, and so on. GPS systems will give a more accurate indication of ground speed as well as indicating your track towards goal. Your vario will give you your sink rate and height. By linking these two systems together, as several manufacturers are now doing, and with a polar curve for your particular glider stored in the vario, you will be able to receive constant indications of your

best speed to fly, either to reach goal or to arrive at the next thermal at the maximum altitude.

RULES AND SCORING

It is important that you study the rules carefully before the competition, and fly in such a way as to maximize your scoring potential. Different sets of rules may well place emphasis on different aspects of flying; for example, one set may only give really good points to the first person to goal, while other rules may give almost equal points to all who reach goal, regardless of time taken. Clearly, it is worth the risk of landing just short of goal once or twice in the first case (as you will still get most of the available distance points) to improve your chances of the big win. However, there is no point taking any chances in the second case, as the benefits will be small compared to the risks.

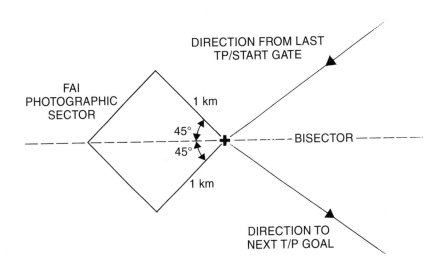

Fig 83 FAI photographic sector

8 Tandem Flying

INTRODUCTION

In the past few years, tandem flying has become very popular. Most of the tandem wings available are scaled-up versions of established advanced or intermediate canopies, with a level of performance similar to that of a good intermediate. They are no longer too heavy to control, but there is an appreciably bigger wing area (normally more than 40 sq m), longer lines, and a greater wing span than a solo flyer is used to. Add to this the problem of having a passenger attached to you and you can appreciate why special

Fig 84 Tandem flying

techniques and training are required to be able to fly tandem gliders safely. There are also the extra responsibilities of flying two up, and specific legal considerations.

BASIC TANDEM FLYING

Set-Up

The normal system when tandem flying has the pilot sitting behind, and slightly above, the passenger. This has certain advantages and disadvantages. Both occupants can reach the controls reasonably easily, and the pilot is kept warm by the passenger, and can still see where he is going. The disadvantage is that the pilot has to have the passenger between his knees, which is often uncomfortable when using a standard harness.

There are two systems in common use for supporting the two harnesses from the single set of risers. Spreader bars have the advantage of being more comfortable in the air, although they are more cumbersome on the ground; V tabs tend to pull the pilot and passenger together in the air, which can get very uncomfortable, no matter how friendly your passenger.

Spreaders have become almost standard now, but most of the techniques described here will work equally well with both set-ups.

Briefing the Passenger

For elegant tandem flying, the pilot and passenger must work as a synchronized team. This is especially important on the ground, where things are difficult enough without having the passenger working against you. Good complete briefings are vitally important, especially if the passenger is inexperienced and/or the conditions are not ideal. You must be sure that the passenger knows what might happen at any particular time, and what they might be required to do. One of the advantages of tandem is that you need not brief on every landing option before take-off, as you can do this easily once in the air, but you must brief completely on ground handling and take-off procedure before you start.

Briefing Ground Crew

It is nice to enlist the help of some of the others on the hill to act as ground crew. It is useful during take-off, especially if you are forward-launching in a bit of a breeze, to have one, or perhaps two anchors, and it is also really useful after top landing to have a couple of people help deflate the glider.

It is a good idea to have any prospective ground crew listen to you briefing the passenger. This gives them a general idea of what is going on, and what you expect to happen. The special briefing you give them must include where you want them to hang on, how much resistance you want them to provide, and what to do if things do not go exactly to plan. Do not forget to thank them as you depart.

Briefing for top landings will depend on whether the ground crew is there specially, or if you are using other pilots who just happen to be there that day. If you have a dedicated ground crew, brief them to keep an eye on you in the air and to be on hand when you land. Again, brief them on what you expect them to do, both when things go according to plan and when they do not. If you are just using the pilots who happen to be about, you will have to land within talking distance, and brief them to come over and

give you a hand after you have landed, before you deflate the wing. One of the nice things about most tandems is that they are very forgiving wings, so it is quite easy to stand on the ground with the wing above your head while you talk to your ground crew.

Checks

When flying tandem there are at least twice as many buckles and odd bits of webbing, so checking is very important. It is also possible that your passenger has no real idea of what things should look like when fixed properly, or incorrectly, so do not rely on him to do his own checks.

Do's and Don'ts

- Ensure that everything that could possibly need checking is checked.
- Never have the passenger attached to the glider without you being clipped on.
- Never leave the passenger to do his own checks.
- Never let the passenger's keenness, disappointment or cajoling persuade you to fly if you are unsure of the conditions.

More Precise Briefing

The more paragliding experience your passenger has, the less complete your briefing needs to be. It is your job to assess exactly how comprehensive a briefing you give them, but it is very important that, especially with an inexperienced passenger, they know enough to enable you to fly safely, and to get the maximum from the flight.

It is your responsibility to assess the passenger, and to ensure that they are all right to fly. You must check that they are reasonably fit and not suffering from the effects of drink or drugs, and that they are keen to fly, and will benefit from the experience. If this is all OK, check their weight, to make sure your combined weight is within the canopy's weight range, that they are suitably attired (with proper boots and clothing), and that the harness and helmet fit them correctly. If they are young, make sure that you have permission from a parent or carer.

Give an inexperienced passenger some idea of the theoretical side of gliding flight, and how a paraglider works. Hopefully, there will be other gliders on the hill when you plan to fly; use them as examples to explain basic aerodynamics, and micro-meteorology. The passenger is probably nervous, so explain enough to reassure, not to frighten.

Get you and the passenger harnessed up and practise some take-offs, with the spreaders attached, but not the glider. Make sure that the passenger is familiar with the workings of the harness, which bits they are able to hang on to, and which bits they must not touch. Warn and show them how the glider will pull both of you around a little during launch, which way you want them to turn, and where you would like them to keep their arms. Emphasis to them that they must try to stay on their feet throughout the take-off, and listen for your commands (for example, run', stop', and so on), and know what each command implies.

Assess which method of inflation and take-off you are likely to employ, and practise this; it is a good technique if you hang on to the part of the spreader where the riser attaches, and apply pressure in the way the canopy would if it was attached. If you are planning a forward launch try running together, either side by side or fore and aft. Instruct the passenger which foot to start the run with, so that the two of you are in step. If you are doing a reverse launch, remember that the glider is likely to pull you both up the hill a bit, and also perhaps sideways; try to simulate this so

that the passenger feels something of the pulling that might occur.

Much of the precise briefing for the flying can be done during the flight, but you do need to tell your passenger how to sit back in the harness, where to have their hands and arms, and how to sit up in the harness for landing, before you take off. Warn them if you are going to take off and immediately turn along the ridge and try to get them to lean with the turn to help the steering. Explain roughly what your flight plan is, where you hope to pick up the best lift (if there is any), and how high you think you might be able to go.

If you feel happy that the passenger is aware of all the various things that could happen, and that conditions are suitable, attach the glider, and re-brief for take-off and flight.

LAUNCH METHODS

There are various launch methods in common use, including two variants of the normal forward launch, any number of reverse methods, and a 'sideways' method, which is probably the most commonly used.

There is also one set-up variation that is possible if the passenger is reasonably experienced, and that is with their arms in front of, or outside the risers during ground handling. It is important that the passenger is well aware of what is going on if you do use this option, as they will leave the ground in this configuration (hanging out of the front of the harness); this can be very disconcerting for a novice. There are significant advantages for setting things up this way; it is more comfortable for the passenger, and also makes the take-off easier all round.

Normal Forward Launch

This is virtually the same in tandem as a solo forward launch, except that, once the glider

Fig 85 (a) Tandem launch

Fig 85 (b) Tandem launch

is inflated, you have the difficulty of running with the passenger immediately in front of you.

Lay the glider out neatly, as you would any wing; if the wind is light, do this without being clipped in, if it is a little stronger, do it with just you attached. Clip the passenger in, check all the buckles (the passenger's and your own), arrange the risers in the normal way, and prepare to launch. As the glider inflates, brief the passenger not to pull too hard, as this can hold the glider in a semi-stalled position. Keep a good push on the front risers until the wing is properly above your head, and then get the passenger to run off the hill. If the passenger has their arms out of the risers, they can put a considerable effort into this; the timing has to be perfect, but it does have the effect of picking the pilot up very quickly, and you will need to do very little running yourself.

This take-off method works really well if there is a gentle breeze, and the pilot is not too much heavier than the passenger.

Side by Side Forward

This launch is virtually the same as the normal forward launch, except that, once the glider is up, the pilot moves sideways, enabling both occupants to have an unimpeded run. Once in the air you will have to manoeuvre the passenger in front of you before you are able to get comfortable in the harness.

This launch method works best when there is no wind, or when the launch run is across awkward terrain.

Standard Sideways Launch

This is the most common launch method when the conditions are soarable, as is mostly the case in the UK.

Set-Up

It is often easier when setting up to have the pilot and passenger attached together via the spreaders, before attaching the glider. If the conditions are not too blowy, arrange the canopy as a good wall, and then attach the risers to the spreaders.

Check very carefully that you have the canopy attached the correct way around; when you are sideways to the glider, it is easy to get everything mixed up. With the passenger turned downhill, and you facing uphill, the risers fall easily to hand and it is reasonably simple to pull the glider up. As you really do not want to let go of the controls at any time during the launch, it is imperative that you set up with the brakes in the correct hands. Check again that everything is the right way around, especially the brakes, and you are ready to go.

Launch

If the wind is a little on the strong side and you feel that help would be advantageous, ask your ground crew to hang on to the front of the passenger's harness. They can then prevent the passenger being pulled off his feet, and will be in a good position to see the glider and guide the passenger underneath the middle.

It is likely that, especially with a good anchor, the glider will try and over-fly you. Be ready to apply full brake to stop it collapsing as it gets overhead. Fortunately, most tandem wings are very forgiving, so do not give up on it until it is really beyond recovery. You might want to position someone behind the wing to catch the wreckage, though.

Once the glider is inflated successfully, there is no need immediately to run off the hill; the glider should sit there quite happily in even light winds. Brief your passenger well on when you plan to take off, otherwise they may try to run off the hill as soon as the anchor releases. If the passenger is very light, they might feel that the glider is already supporting their weight, even when stationary. Do not let them pick their feet up unless you plan to take off straight away; if the wind drops slightly, you will quickly find the whole weight of the passenger on your shoulders.

Reverse Launch

There are various ways of setting up for a reverse launch, but they are all, generally, inferior to a well-executed sideways launch. The one exception is when you have a small, light, experienced passenger. A technique that works well in this case is to have the passenger reversed as well as the pilot. With you both standing facing up the hill, and the spreaders arranged appropriately, it is very simple to inflate the glider, even in a strong wind with no assistance. The problem is that the passenger has to duck underneath the spreader to face the front (hence the restriction on size as well as experience). Unlike when solo flying, there is no unwinding force

on the passenger, so it takes some thought for them to turn back in the correct direction. A good tip is to get the passenger to hang on to the spreader under which they need to duck, so that, as it comes up, they know which way to turn.

IN FLIGHT

The first thing that you are likely to notice as you take off is that you will need more speed to lift off successfully. Resist the temptation to apply too much brake in order to launch, although more than is normal on a solo glider is quite acceptable. Be very careful, though, as the brake position could well be a lot higher than you are used to (due to the spreaders and short risers); the passenger also acts as a windshield, diminishing your feel for the airspeed.

Once safely in the air, talk to the passenger to describe what is going on, what you are likely to do, and what the passenger can do to make him or herself more comfortable. The passenger does not need to hang on to

Fig 86 Tandem flying

anything, so they can easily manoeuvre themselves into the harness; however, they might be reluctant to let go of the spreaders or harness straps, especially on their first flight. Try to get them to relax and be as comfortable as possible; an uncomfortable passenger can be a real problem when landing.

If you are instructor-rated, as well as tandem-rated, you are allowed to hand over the controls to the passenger. If you do this, get the passenger to practise a couple of gentle turns so they feel how heavy and unresponsive the brakes are. As long as they seem reasonably relaxed, you can sit back and enjoy being driven around. Keep a good eye open, especially when flying in crowded airspace as tandems do not turn very easily, and weaving in and out of other paragliders is best left to an experienced pilot.

The visibility from the rear seat when flying tandem is not always very good, especially if you have a lightweight passenger and spreaders. It is not a serious problem; you just have to look out sideways. If the passenger is slightly below you, the view is much better, but the chance of the passenger's helmet hitting you in the face is increased. Wear a full-face helmet whenever you fly tandems.

LANDING

Approach

As with all landing approaches, allow yourself plenty of time and space to arrange things. Make sure your passenger has his feet down, that you have plenty of airspeed, and that you are going to arrive somewhere near your intended spot when you are next close to the ground.

Light Wind

If you are landing in light wind, you will need a high, firm flare to get rid of all the excess airspeed. The exact height you require will

Fig 87 Tandem, in flight

depend a lot on the wing loading, so think about your combined weight and flare accordingly. Even a few kilos difference is quite noticeable. Tandem gliders tend not to convert as well as high-performance gliders, although a good 'swing through' approach will often yield satisfactory results. Because the wing is so huge it is quite safe to err on the high side when you flare: if you are close to stationary and still three feet off the ground, the drop will be very gentle. Do not overdo it, though.

You will also probably need to take a wrap or two of the brakes to get the glider to flare properly; even then, some tandems will make you feel as though you are holding your whole weight up on your arms as the brakes get towards the bottom. Gloves are essential.

Stronger Winds

In stronger winds, especially if hillside landing, you will need to brief your passenger well on running as you land. Co-ordinating your steps is desirable, so get the passenger to put the same foot forwards as you do. If you do plan a hillside landing, again you need to be ready to flare very early and let the wing drift towards the hill as it stalls. As soon as you are down, fly the wing sideways on to the hillside. Do not let it drop downhill, with the risk of pulling either you or your passenger off balance.

Top landings are simplest of all, and just like a normal solo landing.

Collapsing the Wing

The fun really starts when you attempt to collapse a tandem glider. It seems much more prone to over-flying than a solo wing, when landing in nil wind. Fortunately, the tandem glider does not hit the ground at any speed, so there is little chance of damage. The only

way to stop the over-flying is to co-ordinate with your passenger so that you both run gently forwards just as you land. This will probably work well with an experienced passenger with whom you have flown often, but it is possibly not worth the effort with a first-timer. Try to stay on your feet, and ensure that the passenger does as well; passengers seem keen to keep their feet off the ground as long as possible. All the other pilots on the hill will be watching closely, expecting you to fall over, so take care.

Top landing, even in light winds, can pose a real problem when it comes to collapsing the glider. There are three reasons for this. First, the bigger wing generates quite a lot of drag when at 90 degrees to the airflow. Second, most tandems have short risers, and normally only three to a side, so collapsing on the C risers alone is not possible. Rear-riser collapses always take longer than C risers do, so the increased drag is there for longer. Last, and most important, if you have an inexperienced passenger attached, you cannot easily turn around to face the glider. (If you have an experienced passenger and have carried out a 'duck under' reverse launch, it is simple – with practice – for you both to turn.) Collapsing a big wing with just the rear risers, without turning around, is nearly impossible to do with any elegance.

Should there be plenty of experienced help around on the hill, use it. Ask a couple of other pilots to hang on to a rear riser each and pull hard; better still, as long as there is no chance of inadvertently taking off again, give them a brake handle each. If they run forwards and pull the brakes on by at least a couple of metres, then the wing will collapse quickly. This has an added advantage: if you and your passenger should fall over, the brakes will be applied automatically, and the glider will not drag you.

If there is no help around, some co-ordination with your passenger will be necessary. One way is to brief them to turn around and start to run towards the wing as you try to collapse it. Hopefully, you will be able to hold the wing above your heads until everything is clear, and also while your passenger turns. It is a good idea to get them to put their arms through the shoulder straps so that their arms are not trapped when the wing comes down.

The other option is to invest in a pair of quick-release carabiners and attach these at the centre of the spreaders. Undo the protective covers before you land, and just release the wing as you touch down. Keep hold of the brakes, otherwise you will see your wing disappear into the nearest barbed-wire fence. Sorting the lines out later is not as difficult as you might imagine; pick up all the A lines at the canopy end and work down to the front riser, making sure nothing is crossed over them. With the brake at the bottom and all the As at the top, everything else will fall into place.

RULES AND REGULATIONS

Because a third party is involved, tandem flying arouses the interest of the Civil Aviation Authority. The rules that apply are stricter than with normal flying, especially where 'flying for benefit or reward' is concerned.

To obtain a dual pilot rating, you should have a pilot rating, in the appropriate discipline, and over one hundred hours logged. You need to do some tandem practice (at least twelve flights, including two as passenger), and pass an assessment. If you have no paragliding teaching qualification, this is all you need, but you are not allowed to fly for any financial gain. Strictly speaking, this even includes petrol money to the hill, so be careful. There is no need to have your passenger join the BHPA, as they are a third party, and covered by your insurance, but they are a 'passenger' and are not allowed to take over the controls.

If you have a paragliding teaching qualification (including a TI), you are assumed to be teaching the passenger, so they need to have their own third-party insurance, and to be a member of the BHPA. There is no way around this: according to the CAA, an instructor is never off duty if flying. It does mean, though, that you can hand the passenger the controls, get them to do some of the flying, and charge them for the privilege.

Appendix 1: Air Law

Generally, the airspace in which we fly is split up into two types: controlled and uncontrolled. Paragliders mostly fly in uncontrolled airspace (known in the UK and Europe as 'Rule G airspace'), and the rules governing this space are very simple. We may also fly in some areas of controlled airspace, as long as we observe rules to enable us to see and be seen. Most controlled airspace is closed to paragliders, as it requires radio, and precise speed and height control, for the controller to fit us in.

GENERAL HIERARCHY WITHIN RULE G AIRSPACE

There are four types of man-made flying machine, each of which either has right of way over, or has to give way to, the others. The four groups are (in 'right of way' order):

- lighter than air, unpowered (hot air and gas balloons);
- heavier than air, unpowered (all gliders, including hang and paragliders);
- lighter than air, powered (airships and blimps);
- heavier than air, powered (everything else).

For example, hot air balloon has to give way to nobody; gliders give way to balloons only; Graf Zeppelins give way to gliders and balloons; and jets, helicopters, microlights and Cessnas give way to gliders, balloons and airships.

It is rare, even in the congested skies over the UK, to have any sort of conflict with aircraft from the different groups. It is much more likely that any other aircraft you come across in the sky will be another glider. If a conflict does occur with another glider, a set of anti-collision rules applies. ALL pilots should know these, and fly with regard to them. The rules are as follows.

1. **If two gliders are approaching each other, head on, and a risk of collision exists, both gliders should alter course to the right.**

If both gliders are ridge soaring, the pilot with the ridge to his left should be prepared to move further out, so that the other pilot does not have to fly too close to the hill, or too far over the top of it.

2. **If two gliders are approaching each other, not head on, and a risk of collision exists, the pilot with the other glider to his right should give way.**

The pilot who is giving way should alter course in such a way that the other pilot can carry on flying without having to change course or speed due to the other's presence. Equally, the pilot who has right of way should continue as if the other pilot were not there.

This rule is often abbreviated to on the right, in the right'.

These two rules are the two that affect your flying decisions at all times. In reality, other than keeping a good eye out all round, you fly with special interest as to what is happening in front and to the right. You must give way to any other glider in this area.

3. A glider, when overtaking a slower glider, may overtake on either side, except when they are both ridge soaring, when the faster glider should overtake between the slower glider and the hill.

It is fairly rare for a fast paraglider to wish to overtake a slower one, as a faster glider will normally be well away from the same bit of ridge. However, it is not uncommon for two gliders to get into a position where they are both flying along a ridge, in parallel, one on the outside of the other. The pilot on the outside should be aware that he is trapping the other pilot against the hill, and should be prepared to move out of the way early.

4. On approach to landing, the lower of two gliders always has right of way.

This only applies on approach to a landing; at all other times there is no altitude priority. If a risk of collision exists between two gliders, no matter how different their altitudes might be, Rules 1 and 2 apply. Notwithstanding that, it is good manners to give way to a glider that is below, as the lower glider has less room to manoeuvre, and reduced visibility.

5. When a glider is joining another glider circling in a thermal, the joining glider should circle in the same direction.

Also, the joining glider should plan on flying a concentric circle to the established glider, not fly straight into the centre of the thermal, pushing the other glider out.

General rule: it is the pilot's responsibility to do whatever is necessary to avoid a collision, no matter who is in the right or in the wrong.

GENERAL AIRSPACE

Visual Meteorological Conditions (VMC)

Within most of the airspace in which we fly, we are allowed to fly much as we like. There are certain areas, though, to which we only have access as long as we adhere to a set of meteorological minima that allows us to see clearly what is happening around, and, more importantly, other air users to see us. As long as these criteria are met, we are deemed to be flying in Visual Meteorological Conditions.

There are three sections to VMC, defining the distance we must be able to see, as well as the distances we leave between us and cloud. The measurements are as follows:

- flight visibility must be 8km;
- distance clear of cloud, horizontally, must be 1500m;
- distance clear of cloud, vertically, must be 1,000 feet.

Powered aircraft are governed by these restrictions when they are flying in Class G airspace, above Flight Level 100. Between this altitude and 3,000ft altitude (called 'transition'), they have to maintain the following, slightly different VMC (as long as they are travelling below 250 knots):

- flight visibility must be 5km;
- distance clear of cloud, horizontally, must be 1500m;
- distance clear of cloud, vertically, must be 1,000 feet.

Below transition, and below 120 knots indicated airspeed, these rules are relaxed still further:

- flight visibility must be 1500m (5km if airspeed above 120 knots);

- you must be clear of cloud;
- you must be in sight of the ground.

ICAO AIRSPACE CLASSIFICATION

All airspace throughout the world has been split into seven different classifications, in a system developed in the early 1990s by the International Civil Airspace Organization (ICAO). These are known as classes A to G, and a different set of rules applies to each one.

Class A

This is the most highly controlled airspace, and is totally closed to paragliders, as it is subject to permanent instrument flying rules, as well as certain requirements concerning flight planning, pilot qualifications and ATC clearances.

The following areas are designated Class A in UK:

- Cotswold CTA;
- London CTR;
- Manchester TMA;
- Daventry CTA;
- London TMA;
- Worthing CTA;
- all Airways now without exception. (There used to be an Airway classification called 'Rule 21 (2)' allowing paragliders to cross, at right-angles, in full VMC. This no longer exists.)

Class B

Class B comprises all the airspace in the UK above FL 245, and is open to paragliders. This is of little practical use, as the chances of being able to fly above FL 245 are virtually nil.

Class C

At present there is no Class C airspace in the UK.

Class D

Class D comprises the areas around some of the major UK airports; all traffic movement, to a certain extent, is controlled from each airport. Effectively, all Class D airspace is closed to paragliders, although some local clubs have been able to secure limited access to specific areas by negotiating letters of agreement. Where a letter of agreement does exist, it will almost certainly restrict activity to flying with full VMC.

Class E

This airspace is available to paragliders, as long as they maintain full VMC. The only area of Class E in the British Isles at the moment is Belfast TMA.

Class F

Class F comprises Advisory Routes, similar in size to Airways, but with no exclusivity. They are therefore open to paragliders, but care should be taken within them, as air traffic will normally be heavier.

Class G

Class G is everywhere that is not covered by one of the classifications above. Paragliders are free to do whatever they like in Class G, remembering at all times that they are sharing this airspace with others who have the same freedom. Within Class G airspace there are areas which are closed to paragliders, areas within which we may fly only if we maintain VMC, and areas with temporary restrictions.

ATZ (AIRFIELD TRAFFIC ZONE)

Most airfields of any size have an ATZ (Airfield Traffic Zone) surrounding them. This area is reserved for flying under the direct control of the airfield's air traffic controller, and is effectively closed to paragliders.

An ATZ will be one of two different sizes, depending on the length of the main runway. They are all cylindrical in shape, extending from the surface to a height of 2,000ft (measured from the ground). The radius of the cylinder is 2 nautical miles if the runway is shorter than 1850m, and 2.5 nautical miles if the runway is 1850m or longer.

ATZs are only shown on the 1:500,000 airmap where the airfield in question has not got a CTR. All airfields with a CTR also have an ATZ, so even if gliders are allowed into the CTR there is an (unshown) ATZ that is definitely closed.

CTA (CONTROL AREA)

A CTA is an area of controlled airspace, designated as either Class A or Class D, in the direct control of local air traffic services. The horizontal dimensions have no fixed shape, but vertically they will always have a base altitude, expressed in feet, and a top, expressed either in feet or as a flight level.

CTR (CONTROL REGION)

A CTR is the same as a CTA, except its lower limit is the ground. These two are often in tandem, the CTR going from the ground to an altitude, and the CTA going from this altitude to a higher flight level.

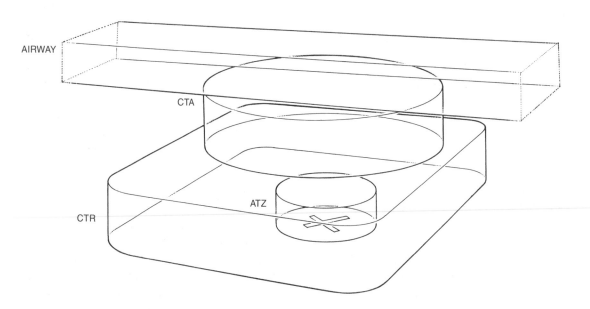

Fig 88 Typical airspace obstructions

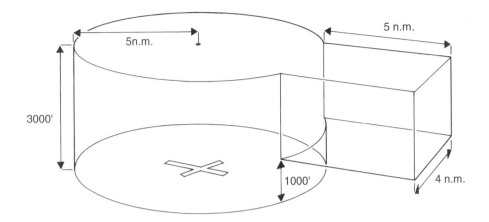

Fig 89
Dimensions of a
MATZ

MATZ (MILITARY AIR TRAFFIC ZONE)

An MATZ is an area around a military airfield, where the military have control. An MATZ is normally of a standard size, but it can have two stubs rather than just the one. They can also be of different shapes, especially where two airfields are close together; this is called a Combined Military Air Traffic Zone (CMATZ). An MATZ will always contain an ATZ.

The standard size for an MATZ is a vertical cylinder of 5 nautical miles radius, from the surface to 3,000ft above ground level, with a stub 5 nautical miles long, 4 nautical miles wide, from 1,000ft agl to 3,000ft agl, normally in line with the longest runway.

Gliders are allowed to pass through MATZs, as long as they maintain full VMC. The ATZ around the airfield is not accessible, although it is often possible to fly over it.

DANGER, RESTRICTED AND PROHIBITED AREAS

These three types of area are normally set up from the surface to an altitude or flight level. Flying is not allowed in them, usually because of some ground activity.

Danger areas are often firing ranges, or missile test ranges; restricted areas are normally associated with passive, but dangerous places, and are not necessarily closed to all air traffic (check locally); prohibited areas are places where there might be some inherent danger to the pilot, where flying is totally prohibited.

All three types of area are shown on the 1:500,000 airmap, each with a serial number, prefaced with either D, R or P. There is a serial number, a slash and another number, which relates to the upper limit of the area, in thousands of feet. For example, D118/10 is a Danger Area, number 118, which extends from the surface to 10,000ft amsl.

Some areas are only active when NOTAMed. Check with the local club if you think there is a chance that a particular area might be open. Be very careful if you out-land in an open Danger Area, as there may be live ammunition rounds lying around.

OTHER HAZARDOUS AREAS

Including free-fall parachuting sites (surface to a maximum of FL150, 2nm radius) and High Intensity Radio Transmission Areas. These are both to be avoided. HI Radio will also disturb your vario from quite a distance, so give these areas a very wide margin.

PURPLE AIRSPACE

Temporary Restricted Airspace, established when members of the Royal family are flying, in fixed-wing aircraft. NOTAMed on a daily basis, as are helicopter Royal flights, which have no Purple Airspace, but you are expected to keep well clear.

Details of Royal Airspace, as well as other Temporary Airspace Restrictions, can be found on a Freephone service (0500 354802), which are updated daily.

AREA OF INTENSE AERIAL ACTIVITY (AIAA)

This is purely an advisory term for especially busy sections of airspace. There is no restriction on the flying, but an especially good lookout is advised.

LOW FLYING REGULATIONS

There are three restrictions to low flying, as follows, depending on the area being over-flown.

1. An aircraft may not fly over a congested area lower than either such a height that would enable it to glide clear, or 1,500ft above the highest fixed object within 2,000 feet, whichever is the higher.
2. An aircraft may not fly over, or within 3,000ft of, an open-air gathering of more than 1,000 people, without the written permission of the CAA and the organizers of the event.
3. An aircraft may not fly closer than 500ft to any person, vessel, vehicle or structure, except when taking off, landing or ridge soaring.

With regard to Rule 1, a congested area can be defined as an area that contains no safe landing places. There are few such areas when paragliding, as most built-up areas contain parks and playing fields large enough for landing. Great care should still be taken if you do end up flying low close to buildings.

With regard to Rule 3, it is unlikely that you would ever be within 500ft of anything unless taking off, landing or ridge soaring. If you find yourself within 500ft of the ground during a cross-country flight, the chances are that the flight is near its end, and you would be close to a safe landing field.

AIRSPACE MAPS

All the airspace information we require is contained on one set of maps, the 1:500,000 aeronautical chart. This is a series of three maps, containing some surface information, overlaid with all the airspace classifications. If you are planning any sort of cross-country flight, you must be in possession of the latest edition for the area in which you plan to fly.

The three charts are:

· UK ICAO 1:500,000 Southern England and Wales
· UK ICAO 1:500,000 Northern England and Northern Ireland
· UK ICAO 1:500,000 Scotland, Orkney and Shetland

The CAA also produces a series of eighteen 1:250,000 charts, covering the whole of the UK. These have an advantage in that they contain much more topographic information than the 1:500,000, but have two distinct disadvantages. First, they only show airspace with a lower limit at or below 'transition' (3,000 feet). Normally, a considerable proportion of any XC will be above this altitude, so if you use one of these charts you would need to transfer higher-level information from a 1:500,000 chart. Second, it is surprisingly easy to fly off the edge of the map at 1:250,000 scale, or at least have to re-fold it every hour or so.

The 1:500,000 charts are updated once a year, on average. If the changes affect the 1:250,000 scale maps as well, these are also re-issued. They cost around £11 each, so keeping up to date is no great expense. Some suppliers have an automatic subscription service, so that any new chart is delivered to you on its release.

If you are using a GPS that contains a Jeppesen database for airspace navigation, you should also carry the relevant 1:500,000 chart, as some necessary information is not included on the database. Jeppesens cost around £75 a year to keep updated, and GPS batteries always seem to go flat at the crucial part of the flight.

ALTIMETER SETTINGS

There are three altimeter setting scales that are used in various instances in this country. They are:

QNH – Altimeter set with zero at sea level (or the pressure set at ambient). This is the most useful setting, as most of the airspace you meet will also be expressed in feet above mean sea level. Easiest achieved by setting the actual height of the hill before take-off. 'Altitudes' are QNH.

QFE – Altimeter set with zero at launch height. Useful when ridge-soaring or local soaring from a winch launch. Of little use any other time. Airfield ATZs are 2,000ft QFE, i.e. 2,000ft above the airfield. 'Heights' are QFE.

QNE – Altimeter set at a pressure of 1013.2 hectopascals. This is 'standard pressure setting' and all Flight Levels are measured this way (in hundreds of feet).

A NOTE ABOUT UNITS

Before metrication, horizontal distances were measured in nautical miles, and vertical distances measured in feet. This had the great advantage that the remote onlooker could tell from the units whether horizontal or vertical distances were involved.

With metrication, the nautical mile became a redundant unit. The foot should have suffered the same fate, but it is so closely associated with height and baro-metric pressure (especially flight levels) that it was decided to stick with feet for altitude, and metres/kilometres for horizontal distances. This maintains the advantage of having different units for the two measurements.

In East European countries metric measurements are used throughout, even to the extent of having metric flight levels. Unfortunately, matching them up to imperial flight levels leads to such complications as FL16.6, and so on.

The above does not apply to 'pre-metrication' fixed distances sizes of ATZs, MATZs, width of Airways, and so on which are still expressed in nautical miles. So, the dimensions of an ATZ are expressed in nautical miles horizontally and feet vertically, but the exact size depends on the length of the main runway, which is expressed in metres.

Finally, the CAA, although it talks in terms of feet and nautical miles to fellow aviators, is supposed to use metres when talking to the general public. This leads to a slightly ridiculous situation where, for example, with a permit (when you are an aviator) you may tow to the permit height, expressed in feet, while without a permit (when you are not a proper aviator) you may only tow to a much lower height, expressed in metres.

Appendix 2: European Airworthiness Classifications

REGULATIONS

The strength and manufacturing quality of equipment, such as paragliders, harnesses and reserves, is of prime importance; the pilot's life depends on them not to break at the wrong moment, and to work correctly all the time. Manufacturers have, therefore, to comply with certain regulations.

Each piece of equipment must be tested for various aspects of performance: harnesses and helmets for strength and adjustment, paragliders and reserves for strength and stability. Different standards have been devised for each, and each will have a separate CE number, representing that standard under European law.

The standards for harnesses, helmets and reserves are simple, and need not concern the pilot much. Reserves are tested within a particular weight range, and it is important that you check that you are well within the correct weight when you buy one. Perceived wisdom seems to be to go for the biggest reserve that you can get, within reason (although, the bigger the reserve, the longer the opening time). If in doubt, seek professional opinion.

PARAGLIDER FLIGHT TESTS

Paraglider airworthiness does pose a particular problem, especially with regard to stability. A paraglider is a unique craft for many reasons, not least because it is reason-ably easy to fly it outside of its stable flight envelope. That is to say, it requires some active piloting in turbulent conditions, the amount of which depends to some degree on the design of the paraglider. Therefore, unlike most aircraft, which can have a universal airworthiness standard, paragliders need different standards dependant on expected pilot skill level.

Various standards have been applied, primarily in France, by ACPUL, the French manufacturers' association, and by AFNOR, the French standards institute, and in Germany by the local paragliding association, DHV. The BHPA has been a co-signatory to the French schemes, and had some input into improvements made over the years, and it also recognizes the DHV *Guterseigel*.

A Europe-wide standard has now been established, combining the best of all the previous standards. Each size of each model of paraglider is tested within one of four possible categories: Standard (gliders suitable for average pilots), Performance (suitable for experienced, cross-country pilots), Competition (suitable for top competition pilots), and Tandem (a glider capable of carrying two people).

A maximum of seventeen flight tests is performed on each size of each model. Whether a particular test is done, and the acceptable result, depends on the classification the manufacturer is trying to achieve. The tests are filmed on video from various angles, and a panel of judges replays the tape to judge whether a glider has achieved a pass for each applicable test.

Briefly, the tests cover:

1. take-off;
2. landing;
3. speed range, using brakes only;
4. behaviour when using accessories (such as trimmer or speed system);
5. pitch stability (not Competition or Tandem);
6. recovery from deep stall, using brakes;
7. recovery from B stall, slow release (not Competition or Tandem);
8. recovery from B stall, fast release;
9. turning ability;
10. manoeuvrability;
11. turn reversal;
12. recovery from an asymmetric tuck;
13. recovery from a maintained asymmetric tuck;
14. recovery from a spin (not Competition);
15. recovery from an asymmetric stall (not Competition);
16. recovery from a symmetric tuck (not Competition or Tandem);
17. recovery from a maintained spiral dive.

Every glider must have a user's manual that includes the following points.

1. The method to be used by the pilot for inducing each test configuration, and the method of recovery.
2. Recommended frequency of inspection.
3. Any maintenance instructions

4. A full specification.
5. The certification standard achieved.

Assuming the glider has passed all the certification criteria, the wing is labelled to that effect. The label must have the following information:

1. make, model and size
2. category (Standard, Performance, Competition, Tandem);
3. minimum total weight in flight (including pilot, harness, glider, accessories, and so on);
4. type of harness used during the tests;
5. accessories supplied (trimmer range, speed system range);
6. maintenance schedule.

If there is no label on the wing, it must be assumed that no certification has been done on that particular model.

PARAGLIDER STRUCTURAL TESTS

Two structural tests are performed on each size of glider. The first of these is a shock-load test, where the glider is shock-loaded to 6000N, and the second is a maintained load test, where the glider is subjected to a load of eight times the maximum total flying weight recommended. On completion of both tests the glider must be still structurally sound.

Appendix 3: BHPA Qualifications and Exams

The British Hang Gliding and Paragliding Association is the governing body for paragliding and, as such, it has been tasked by the Civil Aviation Authority to control all hang gliding and paragliding activity in this country. Its brief includes setting up and running a suitable airworthiness scheme, providing third party insurance cover and maintaining a qualification rating system for all pilots.

The system has one basic pilot qualification, called, not surprisingly, 'Pilot'. Until you have achieved your pilot rating you are deemed to be still under tuition. The first part of this tuition you have to do under the supervision of a qualified flying instructor (QFI); the second part under a watchful eye of a club coach.

There are two intermediate qualifications on the way to Pilot rating: Elementary Pilot (EP) and Club Pilot (CP). Once you are rated EP, then you have shown that you possess a basic understanding and the ability to control the paraglider, but not much else. The CP qualification shows that you have shown good enough decision making and airmanship qualities to be released by the QFI and let loose into the clubs.

At each stage there is both a practical minimum that you must have achieved, and also a theory exam that you must pass. The practical tasks for Elementary Pilot are:

· Demonstrate pre- and post-flight routines (inflation, launch and collapse)

· Safely carry out launch assistance for other pilots
· Demonstrate pre-flight checks
· Complete at least three low level and six 300ft+ flights
· Complete at least four controlled landings in a designated area
· Demonstrate safe airspeed control
· Demonstrate left and right turns
· Describe and evaluate a site and give a flight plan appropriate for the conditions
· Satisfy the instructor as to attitude and airmanship.

And the exam covers:

· Rules of the air
· CAA restrictions on when and where you can fly
· How an aerofoil works and effects of angle of attack
· Airspeed, ground speed and wind speed
· Identifying areas of lift and turbulence
· Dealing with problems in flight
· Basic weather and forecasting.

The CP tasks are a direct continuation from EP. The practical tasks are:

· At least twenty flights after EP, with a ground clearance of at least 200ft. including two flights of more than five minutes' duration
· Successfully launch in light and strong winds

- Demonstrate stable 90- and 180-degree turns
- Demonstrate two top landings within a designated area
- Complete all appropriate logbook entries
- Display an ability to fly safely and competently in the company of others
- Satisfy the instructor as to attitude and airmanship appropriate with holding a CP rating
- Demonstrate slow flight awareness and discuss its inherent dangers
- Demonstrate 'big ears' rapid descent
- Maintain control whilst recovering from tucks of not less than 25 per cent
- Discuss the correct action for avoiding and recovering from tucks, stalls and spins.

The exam covers all the topics for EP, plus:

- Cloud types and their associated weather
- Air law associated with flying paragliders
- Principles of flight, lift, drag etc.
- BHPA and CAA rules and restrictions
- Theoretical and practical aspects of stalls, spins, spiral dives etc.

From CP to Pilot you are, often, left to progress with minimal guidance, so here is a list of the basic requirements for both the practical and theoretical aspects of the Pilot Rating. Make sure that you keep a comprehensive logbook of all your flying so that you are able to prove to the instructor that you have completed all the relevant tasks when you apply for the exam.

PRACTICAL

Most of the tasks for Pilot rating you will have completed in your normal flying, in your progress towards the minimum twenty-five hours requirement. There is a requirement to fly in thermic conditions at least five times (therefore away from the coast), perform two top landings at each of two sites, do 360s in both directions, and also show recovery from asymmetric tucks of not less than 50 per cent. Alongside the more defined tasks you must show a high standard of airmanship at all times, and fly with regard to the rules of the air.

THEORETICAL

The theory exam consists of three sections, covering airlaw, meteorology and theory of flight.

Airlaw

- Collision avoidance rules
- Low flying rules
- Airspace classifications, access and regulations
- All information contained on the 1:500,000 airmaps
- Magnetic variation
- Pyrotechnic signals

Meteorology

- Vertical atmospheric cross-section
- Sections through warm, cold and occluded fronts
- Cloud and fog types, and meaning
- Buys-Ballot law and isobaric charts
- Temperature gradients and lapse rates
- Wind types and causes
- Altimeter settings

Theory of Flight

- Forces acting on a wing
- Bernoulli's theorem
- Stability

- Polar curves, minimum sink rate and maximum glide speed

As well as passing the theory examination, you are required to show a good theoretical knowledge of all unstable manoeuvres and the appropriate recovery procedure.

Although there is no regulation concerning the necessary rating required, you are expected to be Pilot rated before you start expecting to fly XC on a regular basis.

There is one higher qualification above Pilot, which is called Advanced Pilot. This is used as an indication of your experience when applying for specific things, such as entry into National competitions and applying for Senior Instructor rating. There is again a minimum requirement, both practical and theoretical, and an exam to pass. The practical tasks are all cross-country related, and include having flown a 20km+ XC, as well as a 20km+ out-and-return flight. You must also have completed a further thirty-five hours since Pilot rating, though most people will be well in excess of this. The theoretical side is based mainly on the navigational requirements during a fictitious XC flight, and the various bits of tricky airspace that you would come across.

Parallel to the pilot rating scheme there is the Instructor Rating Scheme. Unlike many other sports, where instructing is a continuation from the normal rating system, in paragliding few of the top pilots are instructors, and even fewer instructors are top pilots.

Glossary

3 up (example) Rate of climb when flying within a thermal. 3 up = 300ft per minute

360 A full circle.

Aerofoil Shape of the cross-section of the wing.

AIAA Area of Intense Aerial Activity.

AirMet Short range aviation forecast.

ALR Adiabatic Lapse Rate; rate of cooling with expansion of a gas, normally due to the gas rising, such as air within a thermal.

Angle of attack Angle between the airflow and the wing. More accurately, between the airflow and the chord line.

ANO Air Navigation Order; legal document containing all airlaw.

Anticyclone Area of high atmospheric pressure, normally associated with stable conditions.

Aspect ratio Ratio of the span to the mean chord, usually measured as the span squared divided by the area.

Asymmetric tuck Closure of part of one side of the glider, due to a negative angle of attack.

ATZ Air Traffic Zone.

B-line stall Technique for deforming the aerofoil to greatly increase descent rate.

Beat Flying back and forth in the lift band.

Big ears Technique for collapsing the wing tips to increase descent rate.

Centre of gravity Point at which the total weight can be said to act from.

Centre of pressure Point at which the total aerodynamic forces can be said to act from.

Chord Front to back distance. Normally taken as an average across the wing.

Chord line Line joining the centre of curvature of the leading and trailing edges.

Cloud streets A line of cumulus clouds starting from one trigger or source.

CTA Control Area. From an altitude to an altitude or flight level.

CTR Control Region. From the surface to an altitude or flight level.

DALR Dry Adiabatic Lapse Rate, i.e. lapse rate for dry air.

Deep stall *see* Parachutal stall.

Depression Area of low atmospheric pressure, normally associated with wind and rain.

Flight Level Altitude, expressed in hundreds of feet, above transition, measured at a standard pressure setting of 1013.2mb. Always prefixed by FL.

Front Boundary between two air masses of different pressure and temperature.

ICAO International Civil Airspace Organisation.

IFR Instrument Flying Rules.

IMC Instrument Meteorological Conditions.

Induced drag Air resistance created by generating lift.

Lapse rate Rate of cooling with altitude.

Leading edge Front edge of the aerofoil.

Lift band Area in front of an into-wind slope, where the air is deflected upwards at a speed greater than minimum sink.

MATZ Military Air Traffic Zone.

Max glide Maximum glide ratio, also maximum lift to drag ratio.

Max L/D *see* Max glide.

Min sink Minimum sink rate.

Parachutal stall Stall entered from very low forward speed, where the wing maintains its correct shape, but stops flying. Also known as deep stall.

Parasitic drag Air resistance created by movement through the air.

Pitch Nose up, nose down action.

PLF Parachute landing fall. Way of minimizing injury during a fast landing.

Polar curve Performance curve; graph of sink rate against air speed.

Roll Wing tip up, wing tip down action.

SALR Saturated Adiabatic Lapse Rate, i.e. lapse rate within a cloud.

Span Tip to tip distance; width of wing. Can be measured either flat or projected.

Spin Unstable manoeuvre where the glider rotates quickly due to one half of the wing being stalled.

Spiral dive Rapid descent technique.

Stall Unstable manoeuvre where the wing has stopped flying due to too great an angle of attack.

Symmetric tuck Closure of the centre section of the glider, due to a negative angle of attack.

Thermal Bubble of warm, rising air.

TMA Terminal Manoeuvring Area.

Trailing edge Rearmost edge of the aerofoil.

VFR Visual Flying Rules.

VMC Visual Meteorological Conditions.

XC Cross country. A flight away from launch point, usually using thermals.

Yaw Wing tip forward, wing tip back action.

Further Reading

WEATHER

Bradbury, Tom, *Meteorology and Flight* (A & C Black)
All the weather information you will ever need, with good explanations and diagrams. It is not the easiest read, but very comprehensive.

Piggott, Derek, *Understanding Flying Weather* (A & C Black)
Lightweight weather guide aimed at all aviators, not just gliders. An excellent introduction.

Watts, Alan, *Air Riders' Weather* (A & C Black)
Almost as comprehensive as Bradbury, but with a hang gliding and paragliding slant, and probably a slightly easier read.

AIR LAW

CAP 85, *Air law for candidates for the PPL* (CAA)
Extracts from the Air Navigation Order concerning air law for PPL examinees. Ideal.

PARAGLIDING

Sanderson, Jocky, *Security in Flight* (BHPA video)
Excellent video showing unstable manoeuvres, and the proper recovery techniques.

Index